UNDERSTANDING POLICE INTELLIGENCE WORK

Adrian James

KEY THEMES IN POLICING

The Key Themes in Policing series aims to support the growing number of policing modules on both undergraduate and postgraduate courses, as well as contribute to the development of policing professionals, both those new in service and existing practitioners. It also seeks to respond to the call for evidence-based policing led by organisations such as the College of Policing in England. By producing a range of high-quality, research-informed texts on important areas of policing, contributions to the series support and inform both professional and academic policing curriculums.

Representing the first contribution to the series, *Understanding police intelligence work* by Adrian James does just this. At the time of writing, set against a backdrop of increased fear and suspicion following recent terrorist attacks in several nations, the role of security services and the police in intelligence collection through communities and surveillance networks is in sharp focus. The UK budget announcement in November 2015 saw additional funding directed towards counter-terrorism and the expected funding cuts to police numbers have not materialised. At the same time, there remains continued concern over the proportionality and the power of the state in relation to balancing police effectiveness with due process, civil liberties and legitimacy.

Adrian James is a former police officer and now senior lecturer in criminal investigation at the University of Portsmouth with a history of working and conducting research in the use of intelligence in policing. Although this book is not an ethnography, the value of 'insider' status in conducting research within the field and offering a balanced perspective between official processes and the reality of practice is crucial in presenting an accurate portrayal of the use of intelligence. Publication of this book could not be more timely, and, as the debates raised above take the stage, what the police do and how they do it will inevitably be closely scrutinised. Adrian James has structured his book to cover key areas that will relate to any review of intelligence ranging from theoretical influences on intelligence work through to legal frameworks, organisation structures, intelligence processes, professionalising the field, intelligence failures and challenges for the future. This book will serve as a useful introduction for newcomers to studying police intelligence while offering an objective analysis with insider knowledge to those already working in the field.

For

Melody, Laurence, Gareth and Evelyn

First published in Great Britain in 2016 by

Policy Press
University of Bristol
1-9 Old Park Hill
Bristol
BS2 8BB
UK
+44 (0)117 954 5940
pp-info@bristol.ac.uk
www.policypress.co.uk

North America office:
Policy Press
c/o The University of Chicago Press
1427 East 60th Street
Chicago, IL 60637, USA
t: +1 773 702 7700
f: +1 773-702-9756
sales@press.uchicago.edu
www.press.uchicago.edu

© Policy Press 2016

British Library Cataloguing in Publication Data
A catalogue record for this book is available from the British Library

Library of Congress Cataloging-in-Publication Data
A catalog record for this book has been requested

ISBN 978 1 44732 641 0 paperback
ISBN 978 1 44732 640 3 hardcover
ISBN 978 1 44732 643 4 ePub
ISBN 978 1 44732 644 1 Mobi

Cover design by Policy Press
Front cover image: istock
Printed and bound in Great Britain by CPI Group (UK) Ltd, Croydon, CR0 4YY
Policy Press uses environmentally responsible print partners

MIX
Paper from
responsible sources
FSC® C013604

Contents

Figures

Acronyms and abbreviations

ACPO	Association of Chief Police Officers
APP	Authorised Professional Practice
CHIS	Covert human intelligence source
CIA	Community impact assessment
CIU	Confidential intelligence unit
COMPSTAT	Computerised (crime) statistics
CoP	College of Policing
CPIA	Criminal Procedure and Investigations Act 1996
CPS	Crown Prosecution Service
CSC	Chief Surveillance Commissioner
CSR	Confidential source register
CT	Counter-terrorism
CTC	Counter Terrorism Command
DPA	Data Protection Act 1998
DRIPA	Data Retention and Investigatory Powers Act 2014
DSU	Dedicated source unit
ECHR	European Convention on Human Rights
ECJ	European Court of Justice
ECtHR	European Court of Human Rights
EIS	Europol Information System
ELO	European Liaison Officer
ENU	Europol National Unit
EU	European Union
FIB	Force intelligence bureau
FININT	Financial intelligence
FOIA	Freedom of Information Act 2000
GAIN	Government Agency Intelligence Network
GCHQ	Government Communications Headquarters
GIS	Geographic Information System
GSC	Government Security Classification
HLEUC	House of Lords European Union Committee
HMIC	Her Majesty's Inspectorate of Constabulary
HMRC	Her Majesty's Revenue and Customs
HRA	Human Rights Act 1998
HUMINT	Human intelligence
IOCC	Interception of Communications Commissioner
ILP	Intelligence-led policing
IOCA	Interception of Communications Act 1985
IPP	Intelligence Professionalisation Programme
IPT	Investigatory Powers Tribunal
ISC	Intelligence and Security Committee of Parliament
LAPBC	London Assembly Budget and Performance Committee

LPU	Local policing unit
MoD	Ministry of Defence
MoRiLE	Management of Risk in Law Enforcement
MPS	Metropolitan Police Service
NAWG	National Analysts Working Group
NCA	National Crime Agency
NCB	National Central Bureau
NcDM	Naturalistic decision making
NCIS	National Criminal Intelligence Service
NCAT	National coordination and tasking
NDM	National Decision Model
NFIB	National Fraud Intelligence Bureau
NIM	National Intelligence Model
NPCC	National Police Chiefs' Council
NPIA	National Police Improvement Agency
NPOIU	National Public Order Intelligence Unit
NYPD	New York Police Department
OCGM	Organised crime group mapping
OIA	Operational intelligence assessment
OSCT	Office for Security and Counter-Terrorism
OSINT	Open source intelligence
PCC	Police and Crime Commissioner
PCTN	Police Counter Terrorism Network
PII	Public interest immunity
PND	Police National Database
POST	Parliamentary Office of Surveillance and Technology
PP	Predictive policing
PSNI	Police Service of Northern Ireland
RCS	Regional crime squad
RCTU	Regional counter-terrorism unit
RIPA	Regulation of Investigatory Powers Act 2000
ROCU	Regional organised crime unit
RUSI	Royal United Services Institute
SIA	Security and intelligence agencies
SDS	Special Demonstration Section
SIGINT	Signals intelligence
SIRENE	Supplementary Information Request (National Entry)
SIS	Schengen Information System
SOCA	Serious Organised Crime Agency
SOCMINT	Social media intelligence
SCR	Serious case review
SOCTA	Serious and Organised Crime Threat Assessment
T&C	Tasking and coordinating
Te-Sat	Terrorism Situation and Trend Report
UKBF	United Kingdom Border Force

Acknowledgements

Sincere thanks to Trevor Budhram, Brian Chappell, Nina Cope, R. Mark Evans, Peter Gill, John Grieve, Doug Harris, Nick Osborn, Mark Phythian and Ian Stanier for their guidance, support and invaluable feedback on drafts and for helping me to work through some of the central themes on which the book is based.

Preface

Intelligence work is one of those realms of government activity in which the state entrusts people with exceptional powers for good and ill, powers not easily accommodated in a society founded on limited government, public accountability and the rule of law ... the public may not always know how or when these powers will be used. There is a fundamental contract formed of trust ... we have to be able to trust the organizations and the professionals. To earn that trust they must convince outsiders that the organizations will try hard to stay within lines ... people understand and accept. We need to see that they train people to respect those bright lines, even under terrible stress. We expect that abuses will be rare and will be dealt with in a way that retains our trust. (Philip Zelikow, US historian, lawyer, diplomat and Executive Director of the 9/11 Commission [2011, pp.541-2])[1]

In a society committed to policing according to so-called Peelian principles, support for both effective intelligence practice *and* the robust defence of the rights and liberties of citizens are easily reconciled.[2] A powerful utilitarian case can be made for intelligence work. There are any number of threats to nation states and to their citizens that could not otherwise be neutralised or resisted but the spectres of surveillance, secret policing and the state's unconstrained access to citizens' personal data loom large over contemporary society. Reaching agreement on the appropriateness of the work is by no means a given. That lack of consensus may undermine trust in the policing institution; it is not too much of a leap to imagine that in its absence, the very legitimacy of public policing may be threatened.

The topic of reform seems to have dominated the British policing narrative for decades but government rhetoric continues to suggest that politicians view the organisation largely as unreformed and reactionary; policing remains firmly in the government's sights and ripe for further and more far-reaching change. Yet few doubt the complexity of modern policing. The organisation cannot tackle crime and disorder alone; it relies on the cooperation of citizens and community support. All kinds of challenges – political, practical, legal and ethical – are thrown down. Intelligence is key to meeting them effectively, enabling the police to target scarce resources effectively and to make the kind of cases that can secure the commitment of allies and stakeholders to meaningful partnership in the policing mission.

Although recent high-profile events involving undercover police officers may suggest otherwise, substantially there are few meaningful grounds for questioning the integrity and commitment of the vast majority of intelligence staff. While there always is scope for improving outputs and overall performance, intelligence officers are no more fallible than any other social group; the problems of intelligence largely are not of their making and their work merits support even if the actions of the organisation or the individuals within it sometimes disappoint. Conceptually, that exploration is underpinned by the notion of historical institutionalism. In particular, the narrative reflects on Skocpol's assertion that 'politics create policies; policies also remake politics' (1992, p.58). In the UK, even if its influence today is much diminished, the policing institution has been a significant actor in structuring and shaping political behaviour and has itself been reconfigured by those politics rather than a passive actor subject to the whims of government or the judiciary.

The research on which this book is based relied on a standard social science mixed-methods approach. Data was gathered from a wide range of 'official' reports and scholarly research, primary data in the form of field notes of professional practice, questionnaires and semi-structured interviews with policymakers and practitioners. Specifically, the data was collected by the author while undertaking research into the National Intelligence Model (NIM) (2003-07);[3] from a separate study of NIM implementation in the Department of Work and Pensions, the Driver and Vehicle Licensing Agency, and the Identity and Passport Service (2009-10), which was overseen by the author;[4] from the author's previously unpublished research into investigative practice in England and Wales, conducted from 2012 to 2014 (n=202); and from a separate nationwide study of the UK law enforcement intelligence milieu conducted by the author between 2013 and 2015 (n=119). Staff, past and present, from all levels of the law enforcement community (including chief officers, borough and branch commanders, directors of intelligence, intelligence managers, analysts, intelligence officers and other front-line staff) made invaluable contributions to these studies.

The research identified that many institutional mechanisms worked effectively (or at least were adapted so that they were made to work) and found expert practice and committed staff at every level of the service but any chain is only as strong as its weakest link. There remain weaknesses in the police intelligence chain (some well understood, others not; some the product of internal forces, others due to external factors largely beyond their control). Recent events have demonstrated forcefully that policing needs to improve its intelligence practices and also to make a much better case for them. That means developing its intelligence structures and refining its processes, but even more importantly developing their people sufficiently that their work is worthy of the sobriquet 'profession' to which many staff aspire.

The book aims to give a broad overview of contemporary police intelligence practice in the UK. It goes beyond the instrumental, avoiding simplistic conceptions of right or wrong, success or failure, and virtue or immorality that the work sometimes engenders. Intelligence officers traditionally have relied on informers and 'followed the money', but in the information age individuals' own communications data is proving to be just as important in revealing their plans and motivations. Modern intelligence practice increasingly is associated with surveillance and data management technologies, but human activity remains central to the work. Despite the proliferation of surveillance technologies, the informer continues to be one of the best sources of 'Little Data' (information about the when, where and how offences will be committed that enables the police to frustrate offenders' plans). Practitioners' practical skills, broader knowledge and understanding of the milieu are important, but their soft skills (their powers of persuasion and other personal qualities that help them to work well with others and to make positive contributions that are valued by policy and decision makers) are key determinants of success. Arguably, that is not recognised in a sufficiently meaningful way by the institution.

The book draws on almost 40 years' experience of working in or researching the intelligence milieu and on an extensive repository of primary data. Every effort has been made to present an objective evidence-based analysis, but in places some subjectivity inevitably leaks through; it is hoped that this is not an impediment to understanding. Finally, every attempt has been made to limit the use of jargon. For that reason (and in the cause of narrative flow), the concededly exclusive terms 'police' or 'policing' rather than law enforcement agency (or agencies) are used throughout the book. Consideration was given to employing the abbreviation LEA but for many in Britain that acronym always will be associated with local education authorities. Readers should interpret 'police' as including bodies such as the National Crime Agency, HM Revenue and Customs and all the other public authorities that have investigatory or intelligence functions and that are subject to the kinds of statutory controls on practice currently imposed by the Regulation of Investigatory Powers Act 2000.

Adrian James
October 2015

Notes

1. The statement may be perceived as ironic, given Edward Snowden's revelations about the activities of the US intelligence community and their partners. Nevertheless, Zelikow's words represent an intelligence credo that all of those committed to true democracy and accountability should support.
2. Many of the principles attributed to Peel can be inferred from his writings, but there is broad agreement that they are the product of the writing of historians like Charles Reith rather than being espoused by Peel himself.
3. See James, 2013.
4. See Osborn, 2012.

Foreword

'Intelligence' work by police and other state agencies has not exactly been 'flavour of the month' in public and media discussion for some time in the UK. Since June 2013 the steady revelations by GCHQ (the UK's communications intelligence agency) of programmes to further its self-proclaimed aim to 'master the internet' have been widely characterised as 'mass surveillance', and over the same period it has emerged that a number of undercover police officers were so embedded in environmental protest groups that they fathered children with some of those on whom they were gathering information. Even after new investigatory powers legislation is in place and inquiries into these scandals completed, controversies will continue as to the effectiveness or otherwise of the control and oversight regimes governing the extensive surveillance powers granted to intelligence agencies and the police.

We can be sure of this because the very subject of 'intelligence' for national security and public safety raises strong emotions. For some, it is the dangerous weapon of authoritarian governments and should be resisted at all times; for others, it is the only potential means of minimising the risks of serious public harm that emanate from multiple directions in a complex and interconnected world. As is clear from Adrian James' exposition here, it is certain that contemporary policing cannot be conducted without making use of intelligence, and even the most cynical has to ask whether 'policing in ignorance' would really be a better policy goal than 'intelligence-led' policing. The author not only has long experience as an intelligence practitioner but, crucially, has reflected on the wider implications of the craft and presents an important analysis of the struggles to have it taken seriously. The strength of his discussion is that it places intelligence in its context. It may well be quite a technical activity that, because of secrecy, is comprehended in detail only by insiders, but, to understand its impact in a democratic society, the conditions within which it is conducted must be understood more widely. Spying is too important to be left just to the spooks.

First, important conceptual issues are discussed; these are often wrongly dismissed as irrelevant by practitioners but should be heeded if their activities are to be soundly based on something other than clever software and overdoses of intuition. Then, the impact of the fact that, during the last generation, intelligence has moved from a little understood and largely 'extra-legal' state activity to one located within a democratic framework of human rights and statute law is considered.

Security intelligence operates at various organisational levels – local, regional, national and transnational – and there is frank discussion of the resulting pressures on key matters such as managing the intelligence process and sharing the product. This leads into consideration of key issues, especially those relating to the digital age and the attempt to use 'big data' and social media as tools for collection and analysis. Finally, the ever-present risk of intelligence failure is considered, along with the challenges for policing as it faces up to the future of shifting technologies, changing regulatory frameworks and a sceptical public. This is a concise and lively introduction to these issues that will benefit not only those new to the intelligence business but also those outside who just want to understand what it's all about.

Peter Gill
Honorary Senior Research Fellow,
University of Liverpool

Introduction

Thursday 5 September 2013, Westfield Mall, Stratford, East London, just after midnight. Early evening showers have left the surrounding streets dust-free and black as ink. All the stores are closed but people are still milling around the cinema, the casino and the restaurants. Few notice the black BMW saloon (stolen some days earlier) parked in the ground level car park or the five young men who alight from it. Carrying axes and hammers, the men quickly and purposefully enter the mall. Now they are noticed but they are wearing hoods and masks that conceal both their identities and their anxieties, which for the time being are outweighed by the excitement generated by the prospect of plundering the nearby Breitling Watches store. One man strikes the store front, sending terrified members of the public running from the mall. He and two more enter and smash displays. Each watch retails for several thousand pounds; it will not take long to make the night's work worthwhile. Overtaken by fear, bystanders clearly will not intervene. This is just too easy. In a few minutes the men will be back at the BMW; in 10 minutes more the car will have vanished into that black night. At least, that is what would have happened if police intelligence work had not revealed the thieves' plot and enabled detectives to put in place their own plan to defeat it. The launching of stun grenades into their midst was just the first sign that things had gone awry for the men; the appearance out of the smoke of heavily armed police officers merely confirmed that the game indeed was up.

This attack merited just a few lines in the national press; the men's conviction was publicised only locally.[1] Typically, these are not the types of crime that first come to mind when police intelligence work is discussed. In the modern era, thoughts usually turn to the prevention of terrorism, the policing of protest or any of the myriad ways that the police and the state already intrude into the privacy of citizens. In a democratic society, privacy is of symbolic as well as practical importance but it is a qualified rather than an absolute right. Intelligence work is essential to the police's success in preventing and detecting crime and preserving (that appropriately descriptive and affective term) public tranquillity, whether by mobilising a sufficiently strong force to catch the offenders in the act (as in this case) or by developing strategies that frustrate offenders' plans or at least ameliorate the impact of their offending. That being said, for any action to be considered legitimate, the police must be able to demonstrate that intrusions into privacy are in accordance with the rule of law, proportionate and necessary.

A relatively straightforward example from real life has been chosen to illustrate the critical importance of good intelligence and even better intelligence practice to operational success. Routinely, intelligence officers are called upon to use their knowledge and skills to combat money laundering, terrorism, fraud, white-collar crimes, threats to aviation security and many other kinds of serious and organised criminal activity. In every case – within those broad parameters the crime type is irrelevant (any one of a thousand examples could have been chosen for this introduction) – they collect information (from any number of sources). In the course of validating the information, they must assess its veracity, ensure its source remains both hidden and safe, and take all reasonable steps to corroborate it. They must use it to build a picture of the subject, their lifestyle, criminal associates and habits, identifying connections and stress points in the subject's social network that in turn may present further opportunities for intelligence collection. As the picture develops, the officer may be able to justify making an application to use covert tools or techniques against the individual, which, if granted, may provide the kind of precise information that an operational unit will need to bring the inquiry to a successful conclusion (that is, 'when, where and how' the offence is being or is to be committed).

Throughout this whole process, officers must faithfully log their actions and their reasoning while ensuring that, in respect of the particular circumstances under investigation, at all times their actions are proportionate, legal, accountable and necessary. That places huge demands on the institution and the individuals within it, but even when those demands are met, success is not guaranteed. The complete picture is rarely known; sometimes it cannot be known. That means that the work can be extraordinarily challenging and risky. This book explains some of those challenges and the risks associated with them. In Chapter One, the fundamentals of intelligence practice are addressed. Chapter Two places those intelligence fundamentals in the context of a liberal democracy. Chapter Three examines UK intelligence structures and Chapter Four assesses the legal and procedural framework that underpins practice. Chapter Five analyses police intelligence processes. Chapter Six addresses attempts to focus and direct the work. Chapter Seven analyses contemporary challenges to police success in this context, while Chapter Eight examines what have come to be termed intelligence failures. Finally, Chapter Nine summarises current practice and proposes an evolutionary strategy for change that may presage more efficient and better organised intelligence work.

Note

[1] In August 2014, at Kingston Crown Court, the men were sentenced to a total of 39 years' imprisonment for aggravated burglary. See www.newhamrecorder.co.uk/news/crime-court/westfield_stratford_smash_and_grab_gang_jailed_1_3733100

ONE

Fundamentals of intelligence practice

Introduction

The intelligence cycle is said to underpin standard practice, though it has been criticised as unrepresentative of the real world. Much of our understanding of the cycle and its failings comes from the security intelligence community, in particular from the US community, which invariably is more frank about its successes and failings than its UK equivalent. Deconstructing the cycle against the background of relevant literature allows for a critical analysis of the analytical products and processes used by the police and the barriers to effective practice – what have come to be termed intelligence pathologies. The first step in the cycle, collection, is a very broad term that covers a wide variety of activities. Some (such as HUMINT) are more relevant to the policing milieu than others that rely on advanced technologies.

Theorising intelligence work

Some of the most basic concepts at the heart of intelligence work are the intelligence cycle, intelligence analysis, criminological theory and intelligence pathologies (factors that undermine the effectiveness of the work). Properly managed, analysed and interpreted, intelligence is key to understanding. At the strategic level, though much may be known, so much usually is unknown that understanding must always be qualified. It should never be confused with truth. As much as this book argues for integrity in analysis, intellectual freedom for analysts and intelligence assessments free of political or policy bias, the real-world limitations of those hopes are obvious. Understanding is inherently ideological, depending on individuals' own cognitive schemas and individual or organisational views of the world. In assessing the reliability of strategic intelligence assessments, policy and decision makers would do well to heed the words of a senior US intelligence official that 'Alas, there is no immaculately conceived intelligence' (Fuller, 1991, p.95).

The intelligence cycle

The intelligence cycle's origins are obscure, but it probably was first articulated in a military training manual published in the US. The term seems to have been coined by two senior instructors at the US Army Command and General Staff College, Philip Davidson Jr. and Robert Glass, in their 1948 book *Intelligence is for commanders* (Wheaton, 2011). Their wartime experiences had taught Davidson and Glass that commanders in that period were not 'intelligence conscious' and sometimes even were 'contemptuous of what intelligence could offer them' (Anon, nd). They believed that commanders could only realise the full potential of intelligence if they understood its principles and procedures but that this was by no means a given; it was the job of the intelligence officer to 'sell' intelligence to them and the rest of their comrades (Anon, nd). That cyclical concept was developed and propagated by Sherman Kent, a US historian and intelligence analyst. A significant figure in the history of US intelligence analysis, Kent is credited with founding analytic doctrine and for creating a discrete and distinctive intelligence profession (Davis, 2002; Gill and Phythian, 2012).

The cycle has underpinned all police intelligence training (and it is said to have directed practice) for many years. The College of Policing's (CoP) assessment of it is that it represents a 'cyclical and sequential process that allows information to be developed into intelligence' (CoP, 2014a, p.1). The cycle is a useful heuristic device that can help people to process information, to make judgments and to recommend action. As recently as 2008, police commanders extolled its virtues as the basis for analytical skills in policing, emphasising that their analysts 'should understand the intelligence cycle as it forms the basis of their daily work, which is to collate and analyse information to assist the decision making process' (ACPO/NPIA, 2008, p.11). There are many variations on the standard model (see, for example, ACPO/NPIA, 2008; FBI, 2015). Figure 1.1 is a typical representation. The cycle begins at 12 o'clock with *direction* when a decision is made to commission a piece of research. It then continues sequentially in a clockwise direction to *dissemination*, which may be both an end in itself (delivery of a research report to the decision maker or as a contribution to an intelligence product) and a means to an end (the work influences the decision maker to make a decision or to commission more research and thus the cycle begins again).

Phythian has noted that whereas its validity is now being questioned, for many years any 'intelligence training course, higher education course, or textbook that did not open with a description of the intelligence cycle would have seemed unthinkable' (Phythian, 2013, p.1). It has been argued that in the modern era, technological change and new ways of thinking about intelligence have only eroded the validity of the cycle (Gill and Phythian, 2012).

Figure 1.1: The intelligence cycle

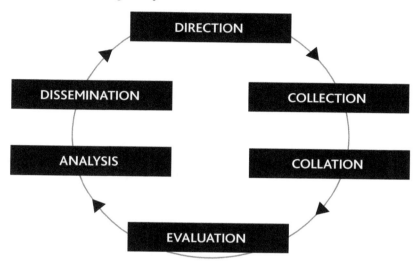

Furthermore the cycle is overly simplistic and its 'failure to accommodate complexity ... has rendered it misleading – a distortion rather than a simplification of reality' (Gill and Phythian, 2012, p.23). Whether the standard depiction of the cycle ever captured the complexities of what in practice is an iterative rather than a linear process is debateable. Hulnick argued that although it was 'accepted gospel' in the US Central Intelligence Agency, the cycle was a 'fairly poor and simplistic explanation of how the intelligence system really worked' (2013, p.150). He proposed an alternative model that fused the cycle with four central functions of intelligence: collection; analysis; counter-intelligence; and covert action. His 'matrix' model identifies two main variables in intelligence: *process*, the familiar elements of collection found in material such as the Association of Chief Police Officers/National Police Improvement Agency practice advice to analysts (ACPO/NPIA, 2008); and *sequence*, which rarely appears in classic descriptions of the cycle but captures how the different functions interact with each other in real-world situations (Hulnick, 2013 p.152).

The limitations of the standard cycle have become obvious to scholars. It has been reconceptualised as 'a continuous process comprising many cycles operating at different levels and speeds [in which] ... tasks overlap and coincide so that they are often conducted concurrently, rather than sequentially' (Davies et al, 2013, p.66). Davies and colleagues' version incorporates the cycle and what are described as the core functions of intelligence (see Figure 1.2).[1] Rather than a single, possibly interminable, cycle, the new model is much more organic, highlighting that data flows in many directions and that the core functions of *direction, collection, processing* and *dissemination* in reality are in a state of perpetual reflexivity.

Figure 1.2: Intelligence core functions and the intelligence cycle

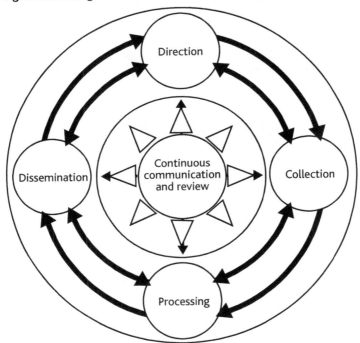

Consider which of the two models this everyday police intelligence scenario best fits; the answer should be obvious, so no prizes are awarded for choosing correctly. A police commander tasks an analyst to research a series of robberies in a designated area. The analyst's initial scanning identifies some of the youths concerned but also reveals that they reside in another force area. Sensitive to policing politics, they refer their findings back to the commander for approval to extend the research. Having consulted their counterpart in the second force, the commander gives the approval. The analyst collects a variety of data from social media and from police records and is able to identify the individual who seems to be the ringleader (that is, the person with the most significant links to members of the criminal group). The analyst consults their commander to seek approval to request communications data in respect of that individual and for static surveillance in the second force to collect more evidence of their association with others believed to be involved in the offences. Having obtained that information, the analyst prepares an intelligence assessment for the commander, but before it can be acted on they receive information that the ringleader's lieutenant has been arrested and is seeking to strike a deal with the police – and so on and so forth.

Davies and colleagues concede that their new model is not 'a perfect fix'. Although it satisfies many concerns about the intelligence cycle, it does so at 'the potential cost of being a much more abstract conceptual exercise' (Davies et al, 2013, p.72). Even though that may be problematic given the dominant action-oriented culture of the police service, if only as a conceptual exercise, the new model represents a very welcome attempt to move the debate on and to provide scholars and practitioners with a palpable alternative to the standard model that is widely recognised as dated and inadequate. Reservations about the utility of the classic intelligence cycle are in part experiential and in part philosophical. The cycle depicts the intelligence process as it might operate in a world stripped of complexity. Beyond the rarefied environment of the laboratory or classroom, life is rarely that simple. Heuristics are useful but limited. In many situations they are necessary and valuable; they simplify decision making, they can support people to make judgments quickly and efficiently, but generally they do not allow much scope for moral or cultural considerations and that may lead to unintended social consequences.

For that reason, a people-focused and customer-centric organisation like today's police service should question the soundness of the intelligence cycle for at least some of its purposes, both in terms of the utility of its ergonomics and its side-lining of those kinds of existential concerns. Some efforts have been made to address those anxieties. The community impact assessment (CIA) process (see CoP, 2014a) aims to ensure that nobody is the subject of unlawful discrimination as a consequence of public policy or of a decision made by a public official. Assessments often are prepared by the police in the context of a critical incident as a way of identifying issues that might affect their relationships with communities. They are sometimes used in operational planning where the adverse impact of an operation on a community is foreseen, but it is doubtful that they are used widely enough to meet the kinds of concerns noted earlier.

Intelligence analysis

Analysis in this context is the tool by which the police organisation makes sense of the social world. Scholars have described it in many different ways, including as 'the translation of raw information into operationally viable intelligence' (Cope, 2004, p.201); as the means to 'provide insights that can drive or support law enforcement investigations, operations and strategy, as well as influencing government policy and decisions' (Interpol, 2015, p.1); and as 'a set of analytical processes directed at providing timely and pertinent information relative to crime patterns and trend correlations ...' (Ratcliffe, 2008, p.93).[2] Tasked with explaining a policing problem, analysts first seek to identify:

- what is already known;
- where data may be found to fill the gaps in knowledge;
- how such data might be gained; and
- the meaning that may be inferred from it.

Fundamentally, at the strategic level, analysis is about using probabilistic thinking skills to discover the meaning of data that often is incomplete and conflicting, and to use that knowledge to support decision making or to provide early warning of threats. Although there is a considerable crossover between the two, tactical analysis usually is more granular, assessing the environment and also the individuals and groups operating within it in much finer detail. The emphasis is on prediction, on targeting offenders to prevent them implementing schemes or on developing plans to reduce crime, often by proactively reshaping the physical or social environments. Of all police intelligence staff, analysts receive the most, and the most advanced, professional training. They invariably hold a university degree and many hold postgraduate qualifications. Typically, UK analysts initially are trained in the operation of the intelligence cycle, using the standard analytical techniques and producing the four key intelligence products.[3] Further training often is provided to analysts according to their role.

In this study, the focus is on network and link analyses because they are central to the work of police intelligence analysts and in that context the most important products are Anacapa (an analytical methodology) and i2 Analyst Notebook (a software package used, *inter alia*, to visualise networks). Even if they have been criticised for over-simplifying complex problems (Innes et al, 2005), in analytical products a picture can be worth 1,000 words if it is put in its proper context. Visual representations have greater impact on the viewer and seem to be the best way of encouraging insightful analysis – the next stage of that process (for example, see Keim et al, 2008).

Today, many scholars describe the development of network analysis in generational terms, that is, as tools and systems that can be sorted and labelled in ways that distinguish between their relative complexity and capability and that also situate their development temporally (see, for example, Klerks, 2001; Mainas, 2012). First-generation tools such as Anacapa rely on manual methods. Tables and lists of raw data, on events and relationships, were used to create link charts showing criminal associations. Second-generation network analysis uses software such as (an updated and improved version of) Anacapa, i2 Analyst's Notebook or similar products like COPLINK or NetMap. The programs manage large amounts of data and provide much richer analyses of the strength of relationships within a network than could be achieved manually. There is a heavy emphasis on the use of visuals to describe groups, individuals and the links between them.[4]

Third-generation social network analysis draws on methods used in the social sciences for many years.[5] In law enforcement, it is used to visualise criminal networks. Network analysis can measure and map relationships and also identify significant individuals within the network (such as leaders or individuals who connect one sub-group to others) who would not necessarily be identified by other means. Arguably, what were described as second-generation tools have now become very much part of the third generation as companies have updated and enhanced their software for competitive advantage and to deliver the functionality that the developing profession of analysis now expects. As powerful as these third-generation tools are, it would be wrong to gloss over the important part played, in developing the tools and techniques that are used today, by those who first applied the principles of cognitive science and ergonomics to the business of intelligence analysis.

In the early 1970s, researchers at Anacapa Sciences Inc. in Santa Barbara, California, worked on a project funded by the California Department of Justice to develop analytical techniques for law enforcement agencies (Harper and Harris, 1975). Building on techniques honed in the field of human factors and engineering, Anacapa developed a system of link analysis for criminal intelligence.

The central purpose of that process was to 'portray the relationship among suspected criminals, to determine the structure of criminal organizations, and to identify the nature of suspected criminal activities' (Harper and Harris, 1975, p.157). A typical depiction of a criminal network using those early tools is shown in Figure 1.3. The figure uses some of the techniques that Anacapa recommended as useful for adding depth and texture to the visual representation of the analysis. It distinguishes between people (circles), places (rectangles), strong links (solid lines) and weak links (broken lines).

Figure 1.3: Simple link diagram

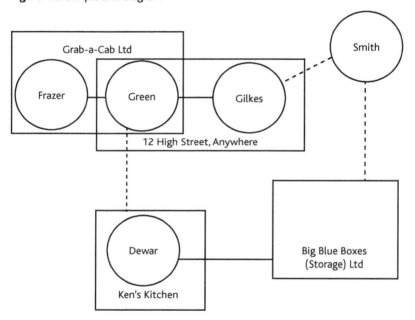

In 1978, Anacapa's early pre-eminence was confirmed by its launch of an Organized Crime Analysis (computer) Program (OCAP). The program was conceptualised as a process of information in:intelligence out. Despite the introduction of technology into the analytical process, the human analyst's inductive reasoning was recognised as no less important in converting raw data into intelligence as it had ever been; hypothesis testing and development remained central to the process (Harris, 1978). That remains true today. The rapid advances in information technology made in this information age may suggest that machines and programs can, or can eventually, replace analysts. It is easy to see how that view might hold sway in a cash–strapped police service, but no matter how much data a program can crunch or how well it can visually represent a criminal network, the human factor cannot be removed from the process. Without the cognitive element (explained in Figure 1.4) and the input of that wider knowledge that comes from experiential learning and understanding of the social context, analyses (no matter how descriptive) are bound to be wanting.

Figure 1.4: The criminal intelligence analysis cycle

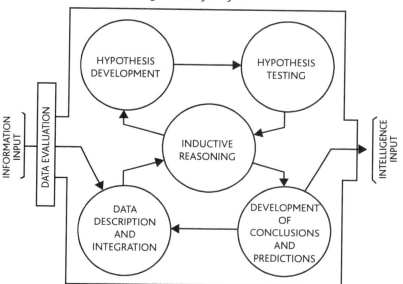

It is largely on the foundation set by Anacapa that network analysis in policing has been constructed. That is not of course to suggest that police officers did not previously grasp the importance of making links between people, place and events; that kind of thinking has always been a key element in investigation. Moreover, systems thinking is a significant factor in policing (even if staff do not always understand it in those terms). Anacapa was the first organisation to articulate its importance and to provide the police with the tools and training to carry out that analysis effectively. Anacapa's influence was such that for many years in law enforcement circles, its name was synonymous with intelligence analysis.

Criminological theory and analysis

Criminological theory should be used by intelligence staff to help them better understand the criminal environment. In some cases, theory can provide deeper insights into the answers provided by the 'what, when, where, why, who and how' questions, which are among the most basic of tools for analysts and researchers. Given the task-focused, anti-intellectual nature of policing, it should be no surprise that the theories that usually are relied on are realist in nature. Realist criminologies argue that behaviour is a matter of free will and choice. Offenders are rational beings who commit crime on the bases of rudimentary cost-benefit analyses; if the potential reward outweighs the potential penalty, it is likely that the crime will be committed. The theories generally employed by intelligence staff are rational choice theory and routine activity theory. Both are right realist in character. Right realist criminologists largely focus on visible crimes that are of public concern (such as violent crime and burglary) with a very strong emphasis on developing effective crime control strategies. Their theories also have been used to explain organised crime (Shvarts, 2001) and financial crime (Gottschalk, 2010). That makes them an almost perfect fit for police analysts.

Rational choice theory essentially is a utilitarian belief that assumes that crime is deliberate and purposive behaviour calculated to meet individuals' everyday needs. Akers has noted that the rational choice literature largely takes 'a strong quantitative modeling approach derived from econometric modeling, which advances our ability to test complex models of criminal behavior and the criminal justice system' (1990 p.654), which also makes them attractive both to analysts and customers of analytical products who value the interpretive significance of numbers. Routine activity theory largely relates to acquisitive crime. It posits that in the absence of effective controls, individuals will prey on individuals or objects they perceive to be attractive targets. Diagrammatically, the theory is usually explained in terms of the problem analysis triangle (Figure 1.5). Simply, it is argued that there are a finite number of offenders and criminal opportunities. Crime occurs when a motivated offender and a victim or target (in terms of property rather than a person) occupy the same space (increasingly, that space may be real or virtual) and suitable controls are absent. Those controls may take the form of a handler who exerts some sort of social control over the offender (such as a parent), a manager (who exercises control over the space, such as a CCTV operator) or a guardian (such as a patrolling police officer).

Figure 1.5: The problem analysis triangle

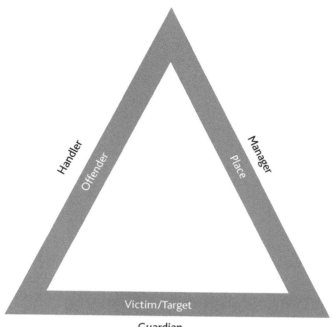

There are of course limits to the explanatory power of these theories. They assume the rationality of the offender when that often is at issue. They are not a good fit for all crime types; they have been criticised as too narrow and deterministic (Akers, 1990, p.675). Akers argues that they are inferior to social learning theory, which shares many of the same features but which also considers the influence of role models, operant conditioning, observational learning and other social factors ignored by routine activity and rational choice theories, and which would be much more difficult to capture in a visual representation.

The weaknesses of these approaches have long been understood. Moe has argued that ultimately rational choice theories are 'concededly unrealistic' and 'not even close to descriptive accuracy' (1979, pp.215–16). They are considered sufficiently useful to the police service to be included in the intelligence management component of the College of Policing's professional practice guidance APP, where they are recommended to analysts as an aid to interpreting crime data (CoP, 2014a). That in itself may suggest the need in the police intelligence world for a more nuanced appreciation of crime causation.

Intelligence pathologies

Organisational failings can often be explained by analysis of an organisation's pathologies. The term pathology usually is associated with medicine and the study of disease. It is used in this context to highlight that organisations function in the same way as living things. Beneath the surface, their sub-systems are in constant flux as they respond to changes in the internal and external environments. A pathology emerges when one or more of the body's sub-systems gets out of sync with the others, impeding the function of the whole. Organisational flaws in the modern intelligence world helpfully have been summarised in that way by Sheptycki (2004) and Richards (2010).

Sheptycki documented 11, largely previously identified, pathologies in police intelligence systems that limited their effectiveness. Those were digital divide (differences between different bodies' data management capabilities); linkage blindness (failing to identify series of events); noise (so much low-grade intelligence in the system that it makes finding the high-grade variety difficult); intelligence overload (in common parlance, the inability to sort the wood from the trees because of clutter in the system); non-reporting (due to poor system ergonomics); intelligence gaps; duplication (two or more agencies interested in the same target); institutional friction; intelligence hoarding and information silos; defensive data concentration (analysis used to justify existing priorities); and differences in organisational subcultures (Sheptycki, 2004).[6] Later, Richards organised those 11 pathologies into three categories: volumes of information (intelligence overload, noise and intelligence gaps); how intelligence moves about (digital divide, linkage blindness, non-reporting and duplication); and cultural issues (institutional friction, defensive data concentration, intelligence hoarding and information silos). More recently, Stanier has argued that an overhaul of the existing legislative framework, the professionalisation of intelligence operative work, and the smarter use of data management technologies may significantly ameliorate those pathologies (2013, p.5). A similar case is advanced *inter alia* in this study.

Sheptycki, Richards and Stanier all noted the police's development of the NIM as a key factor in improving the management of criminal intelligence processes across all policing agencies. Sheptycki highlighted some of the challenges associated with implementing a single process across 'a variegated institutional field' – 43 Home Office police forces, other policing bodies and a host of governmental agencies. (Sheptycki, 2004, p.312). He forecast that 'such a complex set of hierarchies ... [would be] faced with difficult organisational problems' (Sheptycki,

2004, p.313). If anything, that was a gross under-estimation of the challenge the service would face and ultimately would fail to overcome (James, 2013). Richards underlined the limitations of NIM as a vehicle to deliver real improvement in intelligence work, noting that it was 'perceived by most users and observers as fundamentally a management tool ... [rather] than about how analysts conduct their tradecraft' (2010, p.46). It is only now, some 15 years since NIM was introduced, that serious efforts are being made to develop analysts and to improve the business of intelligence analysis. As much as anything, that illustrates the scale of the challenge faced by those committed to achieving professional status for the work.

Dimensions of intelligence collection

This section first examines levels of intelligence before going on to assess some of the different intelligence collection disciplines. In the policing milieu, intelligence enables commanders to accurately assess levels of threat, risk and harm in their communities. It should inform decision making about priorities and options at every level of the service. Intelligence provides narrative and context for real-world events including early warning of new threats that may be just over the operational horizon.

Levels of intelligence

Whether sorting intelligence into different levels is necessary or desirable is moot. After all, one piece of information may have value in multiple contexts. For example, verified information that Charlie Crabtree of 52 The Close is receiving stolen mobile phones is of value because it identifies him as the receiver of stolen goods. It also may be valuable because it might lead to the identification of the thieves; similarly, it may add value to a local intelligence assessment. It has been argued that differentiating between levels 'provides a helpful indicator of its function and helps to scope the resource requirements' (MoD, 2011, pp.2-6). In the military world, that principle is well established. Doubts about the value to policing of differentiating between levels in that way largely are based on the very limited knowledge and understanding of intelligence and intelligence work in the wider police organisation. Attaching labels to pieces of information may only add to that confusion.

The Ministry of Defence (MoD) uses three classificatory labels for intelligence: strategic, operational and tactical. Strategic intelligence is collected in response to government requirements for policymaking or for use in planning high-level operations. Operational intelligence is required for the operational planning of campaigns, while tactical intelligence is very much oriented to the execution of those plans (MoD, 2011). The terms are not widely used in policing beyond intelligence circles and the distinction between operational and tactical intelligence rarely is made. Instead, both are used interchangeably to describe the collection of intelligence on specific groups, incidents or events in connection with the preparation of operational plans and the execution of those plans.

Intelligence disciplines

Intelligence disciplines usually are referred to in abbreviated form. They are many in number, but here the focus is on those most relevant to the policing milieu (listed in no particular order; they are all important to police intelligence work). They are human intelligence, HUMINT; open source intelligence, OSINT; signals (in law enforcement largely restricted to data gathered from the interception of communications and the acquisition of communications data), SIGINT; and financial intelligence, FININT.[7]

It is said apocryphally that prostitution is the world's oldest profession. If that is true, informing for reward must have been a close second in the race for the line. Law enforcement officers have relied on HUMINT since time immemorial. In the modern era, it is the label attached to information provided by informers and undercover officers.[8] For many, informing against others represents the infraction of an unwritten criminal code. Pejorative terms such as 'grass', 'snitch' or 'nark' are usually attached to those suspected of informing, but in the author's experience there is little honour among thieves and that notional code is 'more honor'd in the breach than the observance' (Shakespeare, 2001, in *Hamlet*, 1.4.18).

Individuals are motivated to inform by any number of causes, including the promise of financial reward; revenge; a dislike of the type of offending that they are informing against; and the prospect of a lesser sentence on conviction (Billingsley, 2009). In Billingsley's empirical study (one of a very few undertaken in the UK), of 120 respondents, 66% cited one of the above as their primary causation. As a proportion of the overall number, the single most significant cause was financial reward, with 32 respondents (27% of the sample) naming it as their motivation for becoming an informer (Billingsley, 2009 p.86). Perhaps counterintuitively, for a number of reasons, many police officers prefer dealing with cash–incentivised informers. In such cases, payments are made only on results. That means the informer's motivation is clear and is likely to remain undiminished until they are paid. The bureaucratic demands are fewer, there is a much smaller chance that the informer has a hidden agenda, and finally that kind of risk/reward behaviour fits well with many police officers' views of the world.

The risks associated with using informers are well understood. Too often, informers have acted beyond their brief or officers have conspired with them for mutual gain, either as willing participants or as a consequence of being trapped in a corrupt relationship through their own greed or foolishness (see Cox et al, 1977; Billingsley, 2009; Punch, 2013). Yet, it also is recognised that the best informers are those who inhabit the criminal milieu and inform against those closest to them. Their capacity for betrayal and deceit – essential attributes if they are to achieve their chosen purpose – signal obvious dangers, both for the officer and the organisation, in maintaining any kind of covert relationship with them. Moreover, once their relationship with the police is established, the informer lives under constant threat of exposure. Consequently, there always will be a need for a comprehensive and rigorous informer management regime, one that meets the demands of Part II of the Regulation of Investigatory Powers Act 2001 (RIPA), that properly manages the risks to the organisation and to its staff, that acknowledges its duty for the care and welfare of the informer and that properly considers the potential for harm in using such an intrusive method.

In recent years, those responsibilities have been delegated to dedicated source units (DSUs). DSUs were first piloted by the National Criminal Intelligence Service (NCIS) and introduced across the service about 15 years ago. The central aim was to better manage covert human intelligence sources (CHISs) and to reduce the opportunities for corruption (Clark, 2000) . It also was hoped that specialisation would deliver improvements in outputs and in the overall professionalism of the staff involved in such a testing area of work. The author's research into the introduction of DSUs almost 13 years ago found that staff felt that they had raised standards. Many more officers had become proficient in the application and the number of informers registered had dropped considerably as forces prioritised quality over quantity.[9]

OSINT is unclassified information collected from publicly available sources. A huge variety of data is available openly and very cheaply (which always appeals to budget-holders). Today, collection is not limited in any meaningful way by geography or by time; data largely can be accessed anytime and anywhere. OSINT includes news media, academic and professional reports and studies, public information (generated by national and international bodies, public authorities, court reports, and so on). The internet and World Wide Web (WWW) are sources of almost infinite amounts of data in the form of web pages, user groups, blogs, wikis and social media – all of it available almost instantaneously at the push of a key. For example, a Google search on 'police intelligence' returns about 201,000,000 results in 0.42 seconds.

OSINT alone may be insufficient for a customer's needs but it can provide valuable corroboration of HUMINT or other data obtained by covert means. For example, elaborating on the earlier example, OSINT may confirm that Charlie Crabtree lives at 52 The Close (local voters' register) and that he operates a mail-order business repairing mobile phones (WWW). It also may suggest that he is spending more money than he could earn legitimately (social media). The value of OSINT increasingly is being recognised. A former head of the bin Laden Unit of the US's Central Intelligence Agency claimed that OSINT provides '90% of what you need to know' (cited in Anderson, 2015, p.50). Of course, OSINT may not be accurate or timely. The WWW is awash with lies, half-truths and speculation, so intelligence staff should never take data on face value. Just as with any other collection method, there is the potential for violation of an individual's human rights. That is not the only issue of concern; even when the collection is lawful and human rights compliant there may be a need to ensure that the research does not leave a trace or footprint that may reveal police interest.

In the policing context, SIGINT generally refers to interception of communications and the acquisition of communications data under Part I of RIPA. Interception in this context refers to the interception of a telephone or postal message in the course of its transmission or delivery. Communications data is everything relating to a communication other than its contents. For example, it includes telephone numbers, subscriber details and call durations. Communications data usually makes an important contribution to social network analysis and, in combination with other data (such as surveillance or informer logs), can help analysts to construct timelines and sequences of events. Largely, it is unlawful to disclose intercept material. Ordinarily, it may only be used for intelligence purposes.[10]

FININT is information about the financial affairs of suspect individuals or groups. It can be used to predict the actions they may take, to plan cash seizure operations (under the Proceeds of Crime Act 2002) or to provide evidence in support of confiscation or seizure orders. Good investigators know the importance of 'following the money', but that is rarely a simple task. FININT has grown in importance in recent years and is now routinely sought in major investigations. As the capability of the police to conduct financial investigations has increased, so too has the capacity of offenders to exploit the opportunities offered by globalisation and the digital world to launder the proceeds of their crimes and to conceal their assets from the authorities.

Summary

There is broad agreement that the intelligence cycle is inadequate and does not properly explain how data is managed in the modern era. Analysis has always been an important element in converting raw data into intelligence. The business of analysis is maturing as analysts become more experienced (though the churn of staff is a limiting factor), analytical programs become more intuitive and their products more explanatory. It is no surprise that policing has sought to exploit the development of information technology in this field, but the human factor remains critical to the success of any analysis – so critical that an analysis lacking that component is almost bound to be flawed. Criminological theory can add value to the process of analysis, but is rarely drawn on by analysts. Intelligence 'pathologies' have the potential to limit the success of intelligence work and staff need to be alert to that possibility and guard against it. Of all the intelligence disciplines, HUMINT, OSINT, SIGINT and FININT are those that are germane to the policing milieu.

Notes

[1] See Davies et al, 2013 for a full description of the model and the process by which it was formulated.

[2] Analytic products rely on the application of nine analytical techniques. These are explained in Chapter Four.

[3] Strategic and tactical assessments; subject and problem profiles.

[4] See https://visualanalysis.com/Images/ANB/CHARTS/Polonium%20-%20 210%20Alexander%20Litvinenko%20Murder%201.pdf for an example of ANACAPA analysis and www-03.ibm.com/software/products/en/analysts-- notebook for examples of i2 mapping

[5] It has been argued that they were first used in the field of psychology in the 1930s (Scott, 2000).

[6] Pathologies qualified only where the meaning is not self-evident.

[7] SOCMINT, an offshoot of OSINT, is discussed in Chapter Six.

[8] Since enactment of RIPA, informers have been known as covert human intelligence sources (CHISs). Since the introduction of the Regulation of Investigatory Powers (Covert Human Intelligence Sources: Relevant Sources) Order 2013, undercover officers have been known as 'relevant sources'.

[9] In one force, the number was reduced from 120 to 10; in another, from 110 to seven.

[10] See Chapter Five for further discussion of relevant law and procedure.

Further reading

Gill, P and Phythian, M (2012), *Intelligence in an Insecure World* (2nd Ed.) London: Polity.

Harfield, C; Harfield, K (2008), *Intelligence, Investigation, Community and Partnership.* Oxford: OUP.

Harfield, C; Harfield, K (2012). *Covert Investigation* (3rd Ed.). Oxford: OUP.

M. Phythian (Ed.), *Understanding the Intelligence Cycle.* Abingdon: Routledge.

TWO

Intelligence work in context

Though underpinned by universal theories and concepts, police intelligence practice in any country can arguably only properly be understood by examining its principles, its methods and its social, organisational and legal contexts. That includes probing public understanding and acceptance of that practice as well as well as overseeing and controlling it. Abstract notions of privacy and secrecy are at the heart of debates about the surveillance state, debates that at their worst 'can be polarised, intemperate and characterised by technical misunderstandings' (Anderson, 2015, p.1). The professionalisation of intelligence practice in the UK (long awaited by practitioners) promises to be a positive step in raising the level of debate and removing some of that confusion. There is some evidence to support the proposition that citizens henceforth will see a greater commitment to ethical and transparent practice, but in determining the future of that practice, policing finds itself at something of a crossroads and it is by no means clear which path it will take.

Intelligence work

The quality of that practice is an important element in ensuring that police use their most sensitive investigative tools and techniques, proportionately and appropriately. For the purposes of this analysis, the term is defined widely. It includes the collection, evaluation, management (by human or technological means) and use of intelligence in support of policing activity. It is not limited to covert action or to active modes of collection. As a first option, police routinely should obtain the data they need from publicly available sources, their own organisational memories, willing partners and engaged communities. Only if those efforts do not succeed should covert tactics be considered. Covert methods routinely are used against professional criminals and criminal networks. They may also be used against other offenders but they should never be considered if a less intrusive method is available or if other options would be likely to succeed. The less serious the offence under investigation, the more difficult it is to justify their use.

Translating intelligence into action

Intelligence is important for its predictive value, for allowing police to identify priorities, to fill intelligence gaps, and to develop more effective strategies to tackle crime and policing problems. It often is incomplete or fragmented. It must be critically assessed for credibility and reliability so that a judgement can be made on its usefulness. Corroboration is key to determining the extent to which intelligence should be trusted. The intelligence/action nexus is complex. Analysts may recommend a course of action but they rarely have authority to act. Instead, they must persuade decision makers to accept their findings and recommendations. The quality of the intelligence case is a significant factor in that transaction, but the relative status of the actors involved, the experiential knowledge that frames their understanding of the intelligence picture and even more nuanced issues of culture and organisational control also are important factors to consider. A little-acknowledged factor is that in policing, expertise in intelligence practice largely comes from practical experience. Theoretical knowledge and subject-specific scholarly research rarely are meaningful factors in the development of intelligence staff or in the preparation of intelligence assessments.

Whenever any action that may intrude into the privacy of a citizen is planned, the appropriateness of that act must be considered carefully. The proposed action must be lawful, ethical and procedurally fair. Moreover, the risks associated with it (for the individual or group, community and agency concerned) also must be properly assessed and managed. Fundamentally, the quality and reliability of those plans depend on timely and accurate intelligence, skilled staff and a framework of structures and processes that ensure that the tests of proportionality, legality, accountability and necessity (the standards by which human rights compliance usually is judged) are passed. Adding to that equation the kinds of knowledge and research described earlier would enrich analyses and make them more credible.

Policing and spying

There has always been significant interest in police intelligence-gathering activities, but revelations about the activities of security and intelligence agencies (SIAs) in the information age have brought the capacity and capability of the state to intrude into the lives of citizens into sharp relief. Inevitably, that has influenced how people view the police, who essentially rely on the same tactics to support their intelligence-gathering activities. The dividing line between security and crime often is blurred; today SIAs play significant parts in the prevention and detection of transnational and organised crime, and terrorism. SIAs and the police use very similar methods; there are only so many ways to collect information and the police and SIAs exploit most of them, but SIAs alone undertake bulk data collection and computer hacking. Their role in the day-to-day business of policing is relatively inconsequential. Accepting the realities of that relationship, this analysis considers their work only to the extent that it informs or contextualises the intelligence work of the UK's police.

Intelligence work in liberal democracies

Just as policing has always been so much more complex than simply preventing or detecting crime, intelligence work, which is said to be at the heart of modern policing, is so much more than using information to direct action, as some in the law enforcement community would have us believe (see, for example MPS, 1994, cited in Grieve, 2004). Any critical assessment of police intelligence work, worthy of the name, has to go beyond the instrumental or task focus of the practitioner. Examining the controls, systems, structures and processes that underpin the work can lead only to a partial understanding of how forces operate in this context. One must also appreciate its political, social, legal, ethical and organisational contexts.

Liberties and freedoms

Privacy is a right that is protected in law for European citizens (even though the meaning of the term is far from settled); what is considered to be private differs widely between societies and individuals.[1] Privacy is not just an individual value, it 'is also important for society as a foundation for the common good and for values held in common' (Ball and Wood, 2006, p.93). Arguments about the extent to which the police should intrude into privacy are not simply questions of process and law. They are central to understanding police legitimacy. Intelligence work may be seen to be at odds with democratic principles even when it can be justified under law. The problem may be even more acute in the context of terrorism where the UK has at least made some attempts to ameliorate it. In 2001, the UK's first independent reviewer of terrorism legislation was appointed. That arrangement later was reinforced by the appointment of a special adviser to the reviewer and more recently by the establishment of a Privacy and Civil Liberties

Board. The independent reviewer has not been afraid to point out the defects in the existing system wherever they lie or to whomsoever they may be attributed.

The work represents the Janus face of policing. The endeavours captured by the term contrast sharply with activities that make up the vast majority of police–public interactions that commonly are understood as policing. It often is controversial; there always is the potential for conflict when activities that could be construed as spying on communities are undertaken. For those reasons, policing must subscribe to principles not only of rights and due process but also of procedural fairness. They must not only do the right thing, but, whenever challenged, must be able to demonstrate that they have done so. That requires a significant organisational commitment to recordkeeping and a records management programme that *inter alia* protects vital information, supports decision making and ensures that adequate and sufficient records are kept so as to ensure transparency and accountability for their decisions and actions.

The arrangements described in this book are modern phenomena but there is a long history of covert practice in Britain.[2] From the beginning, the police used the excuse of operational necessity to undertake covert investigation of suspected criminals and radicals and routinely breached individuals' privacy. Brodeur has argued that the necessity of their covert tactics was overplayed and that secrecy often was 'a matter of institutional policy' (Brodeur, 2010, p.35), while MacVean is but one of a number of authors who have argued that secrecy is a product of organisational culture (2008). Whatever the real reason, despite periodically coming under pressure from jurists, the commitment to secrecy largely masked the development of the intelligence apparatus. That prevented meaningful challenge to the expansion of police surveillance and other intelligence-gathering capabilities, which, though lawful, were carried on without the legal certainty that statute or other visible regulation would have afforded.[3]

Statutory controls

Arguably, it was in 1984 in the European Court of Human Rights (ECtHR) that the first meaningful challenge to the status quo was made. In its judgement in the case of *Malone v the UK* (7 EHRR 14), a case involving 'telephone tapping', the court held that the law of England and Wales violated the European Convention on Human Rights (ECHR) because the Home Office guidelines under which the interception was carried out did not have statutory force. Therefore, the interference could not be regarded as one that was prescribed by law, which meant there was a de facto violation of the Article 8 ECHR right to respect for private life. This was not the first challenge to police powers in this regard, but the court's opinion in this case, that the violation amounted not only to a breach of domestic law but to interference with the rule of law, changed the whole surveillance dialectic.

In consequence, the government conceded the need for a statutory framework for the lawful interception of communications and introduced the Interception of Communications Act 1985 (IOCA). That did not necessarily take the heat out of the debate. The Act was criticised for the narrowness of its remit, going no further than required by *Malone*. During passage of the Bill through parliament, it was criticised as 'setting out to regulate canal traffic in the age of the high speed train and the motorway' (H.C. Debs, vol. 75, col. 241, cited in Taylor, 2002, p.69). That criticism attracted further interest from scholars and jurists in police intelligence work and ensured that interception, and covert policing more generally, remained top of many libertarians' lists of concerns.

The Audit Commission's (1993) report *Helping with Enquiries: Tackling Crime Effectively* was a significant milestone in the road towards real transparency. The commission found that the police were 'locked into a vicious circle in which the volume of crime threatens to become overwhelming' (Audit Commission, 1993, p.1). It argued that crime could be reduced only if the police took a proactive approach to crime investigation. More importantly in the context of this analysis, the inquiry team's forensic examination of investigative and intelligence work provided rare detail about the sensitive, traditionally secret, activities of police forces. Its findings stimulated renewed interest in operational methodologies and greater awareness of intelligence among the legal profession, scholars, policymakers and the greater proportion of the police workforce, which up to that time largely had been ignorant of the work.

The commission was highly critical of the police intelligence system, which, despite three separate inquiries in a 20-year period, remained significantly deficient.[4] In many forces, the intelligence function continued to be 'inadequately equipped with technology and understaffed' (Audit Commission, 1993, p.2). Convinced of the merits of the putatively innovative approach advanced by the commission, the Home Office issued a directive to police commanders to make greater use of 'intelligence based strategies such as surveillance and crime pattern analysis' (ACPO et al, 1994, p.117). That found a receptive audience in some sections of the organisation. The term intelligence-led policing (ILP) quickly was taken up and incorporated into the policing lexicon. Arguably, the ILP narrative has dominated policing discourse for 20 years. Though its real impact on policing has been far less than the continuing debate over its use would suggest, the commission's report was revelatory. For example, in its analysis of the police use of paid informers, a neglected but 'highly cost-effective source of detections' (Audit Commission, 1993, p.2), the commission revealed information that had long been kept from public view. That included the facts that:

> One [police] force analysed the use over a recent six-month period of information from registered informants … £60 was paid out per person arrested and £57 per crime detected. For every £1 paid to informants, stolen property to the value of £12 was recovered. Some 219 crimes were cleared up at a cost for the period equivalent to one detective constable. (Audit Commission, 1993, p.39)

The report was a significant factor in the lifting of that Kafkaesque veil, but central government pressure on the police to be more business-like, greater scrutiny of their work in the information age and the occasional scandal linked to intelligence failure also played significant parts. So too has public debate over the evidential use of intercept material and the fallout from the mismanagement of undercover operations (see, for example HMIC, 2014a). The enactment of statutory controls over covert policing methodologies in the cause of securing human rights compliance also contributed significantly to public knowledge of what were once policing's most closely guarded secrets. Consequently, citizens came to learn much more about the reach of the agencies and about the implications of that work for privacy and human rights.

Recent disclosures about the capability of police forces and the security services to use covert means to intrude into the lives of citizens in public, in private, and in cyberspace inevitably have raised fears of the rapid advance of the surveillance state. Those revelations have been a source of disquiet for some practitioners because they threaten traditional practice, but even the most committed advocates of the 'need to know' principle must acknowledge that public unease about the appropriateness of the work often has been shown to be both legitimate and well-founded.

Two recent cases more than most probably have shaken British society's faith in the police to use their powers wisely. In 2010, revelations about Mark Kennedy, an undercover officer working for the Special Demonstration Section (SDS) of the Metropolitan Police's National Public Order Intelligence Unit (NPOIU) led to the premature ending of the trial of six people (effectively Kennedy's co-conspirators) accused of planning to shut down a large power station in Ratcliffe-on-Soar, Nottinghamshire. In its report on those events, Her Majesty's Inspectorate of Constabulary (HMIC) noted that the SDS's recordkeeping was inadequate, with insufficient detail being recorded on 'how the risks of intrusion were assessed and managed' [despite the fact that Kennedy had intimate relationships with a number of people while undercover, and in doing so encroached very significantly into their lives (HMIC, 2014a, p.8). It has been widely reported that Kennedy's colleague and contemporary, Bob Lambert, fathered a child while working undercover on a similar mission, a fact recognised by his employers only in October 2014 when the Metropolitan Police announced that it would make a payment of £425,000 to the child's mother. An official inquiry into undercover policing and the SDS concluded *inter alia* that:

> There are and never have been any circumstances where it would be appropriate for such covertly deployed officers to engage in intimate sexual relationships with those they are employed to infiltrate and target. Such an activity can only be seen as an abject failure of the deployment, a gross abuse of their role and their position as a police officer and an individual and organisational failing. (Creedon, 2014, p.73)

Opinions may be divided as to whether the Kennedy and Lambert cases represent conspiracy or cock-up, even though there may be little disagreement that society and the policing institution itself should be extremely concerned about the individual and organisational failings uncovered. That being said, these events throw up the kind of ethical dilemmas that are unique to this kind of work. It can be extremely risky and officers have to be singularly resilient to manage the physical and psychological pressures inherent in the role. Moreover, it would be extremely difficult for police forces to find an alternative to what has proved to be such a successful and productive tactic.

Of course, successful professional criminals are well aware of police stratagems. They consider police interest an occupational hazard and they can anticipate and potentially nullify the impact of investigation. The challenge for the police in that context is to limit that knowledge by maintaining high standards of operational security so that their intentions and tactics remain hidden even if their interest may be foreseen. It is of course for just this kind of reason that the police traditionally have valued secrecy so highly. Nevertheless, that need to know must be balanced with an appreciation of the virtues of 'daring to share'. Intelligence has little value if it cannot be used in productive ways.

The surveillance state

The now commonly understood term 'surveillance state' often is attributed to George Orwell. In his seminal novel *1984*, Orwell presented a vivid and disturbing picture of unrestrained (and unrestrainable) state control, a terrifying account of officially sanctioned deception, mass surveillance and manipulation of history. Parallels can only too readily be found in modern society. In August 2004, the Information Commissioner warned that the UK could be sleepwalking into a 'surveillance society' (cited in HLSCC, 2009 p.5). Within two years, the authors of a report ordered by that same commissioner felt confident enough in their research findings to assert that 'It [was] pointless to talk about the surveillance society in the future tense because surveillance was simply a feature of modernity' and 'just part of the fabric of daily life' (Ball and Wood, 2006, p.1). Whether in the context of this analysis that is good, bad, good and bad at the same time, or even perhaps neither good nor bad, ultimately is a subjective judgement.

Unsurprisingly, some of the most vocal and committed advocates of surveillance and intelligence have been senior practitioners. Rob Wainwright, Director of the European Union's policing agency, Mike Barton, one of Britain's most senior police officers (and the police lead on intelligence) and, from the security milieu, Ian Lobban, formerly Director General of the UK Government Communications Headquarters (GCHQ), are three among many backers of the work at the elite levels of the police and SIAs. On retirement from his post, Lobban mounted a fierce defence of the role of intelligence in public life. He argued that it was essential that the state had the tools to combat 'the plotters, the proliferators and the paedophiles' to prevent them realising their plans (Lobban, 2014). Wainwright has argued relentlessly for greater information sharing among organisations and countries (see, for example, Sommers, 2013), while Barton has argued consistently for the development of the police intelligence architecture (Armstrong, 2015).

It is a central tenet of this analysis that intelligence work is human activity and that intelligence workers are subject to the same cognitive and behavioural vagaries as any other workers. In that context, Palmer (2009) argued that the effectiveness of Britain's surveillance regime frequently was undermined by human fallibility and that ultimately the incompetence associated with modern surveillance would 'save us from Orwell's surveillance state'.[5] He observed that 'Officials forget to put film in the cameras; they lose the secret data they have gathered, leaving it on trains or in bars; and they frequently never get around to consulting what they do manage to keep hold of: there is simply too much of it' (2009). Certainly, there is some evidence to support Palmer's argument, but the picture he has painted represents the worst of both worlds and no party to this debate should take much comfort from it.

The rapid advances in surveillance and other technologies in the information age should give pause for further reflection on his representation. Just five years on from Palmer's article, film has largely given way to digital media, which have exponentially greater collection and storage capabilities and which provide much higher image quality. Thanks to the revelations of ex-US National Security Agency analyst Edward Snowden, citizens have a much better understanding of the reality of Western states' data-collection and data-sorting capabilities, which are far greater than most would ever have imagined. The extent to which that data either is made available to the police or is used in the ordinary business of policing is debateable, but the mere existence of the kind of programmes revealed by Snowden is bound to fuel public suspicion that they are.

Intelligence praxis

Empirical studies by researchers such as Sheptycki (2004) and Heaton (2010) identified shortcomings in police intelligence praxis. Those inefficiencies (such as the non-reporting and non-recording of information) are by no means unique to policing, but, given the police's power over citizens, they have much greater potential for harm. The police should be challenged and their work scrutinised. Arguably, this is just one more arena in which the continuing battle between the state and civil libertarians over the proper limits of state control is being played out. Waddington described that milieu as 'hotly contested terrain' (2005, p.371). In a liberal democracy, intrusive inspection of public institutions should be both expected and welcomed by public servants. Intelligence work should be subject to the highest degree of scrutiny and challenge. Those are not idealistic or naïve views; forces that accept less are at risk of losing the trust of their communities, undermining the tradition of policing by consent. As O'Neill commented in her discourse on the lack of trust in public institutions, it 'is hard earned and easily dissipated. It is valuable social capital and not to be squandered' (2002, p.2).

Practitioners may argue that the kinds of failings revealed by the cases discussed here are few and far between. The raw data supports that claim, but undoubtedly there is room for improvement. For most forces that means: improving their selection and training regimes to use their greatest assets, their people and their information, in ethical, procedurally fair and productive ways; winning support for their work through greater transparency; making the case for it to stakeholders and communities by articulating solutions to social problems that acknowledge the limitations of the policing institution in that regard; and celebrating intelligence successes whenever possible so that the narrative of failure that often is associated with the work may be reshaped.

Change is always difficult, particularly when it relies on the reallocation of scarce resources, human or otherwise, or when it threatens established discourse or practice. Policing can and should develop more efficient, effective and ethically sound intelligence practices and should recognise the need to better explain the case for intelligence work to a generally supportive but increasingly suspicious public. In summary, 'the task … is to build higher fences around fewer secrets, limiting protection only to sources and methods that merit it, while disclosing as much as possible of everything else' (Gries, nd). Whether that can be achieved is as much a question of their leaders' vision, and organisational culture as it is of resources, structures or external influences.

Reconciling principles with praxis

One instinctively feels that the pragmatic reality is that the police need effective intelligence systems to help them prevent and detect crime, maintain security and manage risk effectively enough to keep communities safe. Even Kafka, one of the most celebrated critics of overpowering state bureaucracy, recognised that people often look to it to protect them from those who seek to do them harm (see, for example, Kafka, 1946). Much less certain is the way in which a consensus on the proper limits of police intelligence work in Britain may be achieved. Agreement is dependent on a multitude of politically, socially, geographically and culturally contingent factors. Cutting across all of those factors is the issue of trust in public institutions and professionals, which (as O'Neill, 2002 and others have argued) seems to be in very short supply in the modern era.

Policing, in that same spirit of pragmatism, has motivated its officers to use guile to push up against the limits of legality (see Grieve, 2004 and Hogan-Howe, 2011). That may extend the parameters of what is considered acceptable, but also may bring them into conflict with the law and with the communities they serve; see the judgement in *R (on the application of Chatwani and others) vs NCA and Birmingham Magistrates' Court* [2015] EWHC 1283 (Admin) for a very recent example of the consequences of getting that balance wrong. The police are bound by the rule of law, but despite the rhetoric about operational independence, policing is inherently political. Its leaders are no more immune from political, social and organisational pressures than any other public sector professionals. That pressure is bound to influence action.

Intelligence work stimulates the greatest controversy when it involves an intrusion into privacy by covert means, which is perceived as unjustified (as in the Kennedy and Lambert cases). Often, judgements on the appropriateness of those acts are made long after the event in courts of law or of public opinion. These are usually determined by a subjective assessment based on myriad factors, many of which (at least to the intelligence practitioner) may challenge logic. That is not to diminish the importance of public opinion. It is rare that the public holds one unified view, but the police need to be sensitive to shifts in the prevailing mood and to be as open about their intelligence activities as need-to-know principles allow. They must accept real oversight (something that notably was lacking in the cases described earlier – see HMIC, 2014a) and encourage new insights into their work so as to better counter the bias of hindsight, which can limit organisational learning and discourage innovation.

Intelligence work polarises opinion. The inherent contradictions in this discourse may never be resolved, but the ubiquity of surveillance in today's society, and the state's increasing reliance on it (rather than on more expensive human and physical resources) as a means of controlling the criminal element in an increasingly distrustful and suspicious public, confirms the absolute necessity of extending the current debate. Albeit that in his writings Orwell principally had in mind the kinds of totalitarian regimes found in Nazi Germany and Communist Russia, *1984* remains just as politically, socially and culturally relevant today. It should serve as a warning to everyone, not least police officers, about the consequences for society when trust in its public servants and institutions is lost.

Professionalising intelligence work

Since the establishment of the first national unit in Britain in 1960, the intelligence apparatus incrementally developed its focus from what Brodeur (1983) termed the 'high policing' function (intelligence activity against threats to national security) and now extends into every level of public policing. Subject only to internal control, the police have used covert methods for many years. Initially, use of more sensitive methods (such as listening devices) were limited to specialist units combatting organised crime, but (the facility to intercept communications aside) they have been rolled out to local policing units (LPUs) so that they are available to support the investigation of a wide range of offences (even if in practice they are used patchily and inconsistently).[6] Although the methods central to it largely developed in a closed world, unfettered by law or external regulation, intelligence practice now is underpinned by a framework of legislation, codes and directions.

That structure was built in a piecemeal fashion, largely as a way of legitimising activities judged by central government to be politically unpopular or by the ECtHR to be contrary to human rights principles. The resourcing of intelligence units and the selection and training of intelligence staff has been similarly disjointed, although there seems now to be more energy in the police service behind moves to professionalise both its processes and its intelligence staff.

Authorised Professional Practice (APP)

APP is overseen by the CoP (the professional body for policing in England and Wales, which replaced the National Police Improvement Agency, NPIA). It covers a wide range of policing activities and represents the official, most up-to-date source of knowledge about policing practice. It is an online resource subject to access control, but with a public version that may be accessed by anyone. A second level contains restricted guidance that may be accessed only by internal users. There are plans for a third level containing confidential guidance that may be accessed only by designated users (often with a higher level of security clearance) but those have not yet been progressed. Therefore, although APP contains a substantial body of knowledge and guidance on an increasingly wide range of topics, it is not yet the single, access-controlled, repository of policing knowledge that was envisaged.

In the context of this analysis, the most relevant section is the Intelligence Management APP (CoP, 2015a). In common with the other APP material, the intelligence section represents a distillation of the pre-existing professional guidance, amended and updated to take account of changes in legislation or policy or as a consequence of the discovery of better practice. Unusually, intelligence work is underpinned by a Code of Practice issued by the Secretary of State for the Home Office. The code clarifies the responsibilities of chief officers and Police and Crime Commissioners (PCCs) in applying the National Intelligence Model (NIM) and also sets out basic principles and minimum standards for managing intelligence (see James, 2013). The code owes its existence to the lobbying of ministers by the now defunct Association of Chief Police Officers (ACPO) in the cause of securing service-wide support for the NIM. The model has undergone significant change. Much of its detail, which initially caused so much confusion beyond the intelligence world, has been removed. For example, more than 150 minimum standards have now been whittled down to just three. In a sense, what is left represents little more than basic information-management principles, but the police's need to comply with the statutory code will ensure that the NIM label will continue to be affixed to police intelligence policy even if intelligence practice has, to all intents and purposes, moved on from it its original incarnation.

Intelligence Professionalisation Programme (IPP)

In recent years, the loudest calls for the professionalisation of the work have come from intelligence staff. Frustrated by organisational inertia, they have been among the most vocal advocates of change. The National Analysts Working Group (NAWG) has been in the vanguard of that movement. Its case for the development of national occupational standards (similar to the Professionalising Investigation Programme that was introduced for detective work – see, for example, Stelfox, 2009) has been assisted by the recognition that in this age of public sector austerity, policing has to get smarter in its use of resources (Winsor, 2012). To be overseen by the CoP, IPP will create a national curriculum for intelligence that leads to professional and academic qualifications that support new opportunities for career development (or at least that is the hope).

The expectation is that standardising professional qualifications across the sector will mean that analysts can develop their career by moving between various public institutions (such as the police, the UK Border

Force [UKBF], HM Revenue and Customs, immigration services). In the process, they will develop a wider range of skills than currently is possible and deliver benefits for employers in terms of agency interoperability and partnership working. New relationships are being forged with higher education by ACPO's replacement, the National Police Chiefs' Council (NPCC), and the CoP. Practitioners will be encouraged to study intelligence to Master's degree level and beyond. Without very much prospect of financial support from practitioners' employers in this budget-conscious era, however, it remains to be seen if that aspiration can be realised fully enough to have much impact on the overall standard of practice.

Police Code of Ethics

The theme of ethics runs throughout the book; not least, because intelligence work challenges preconceptions of right and wrong: virtue and vice. Though a case can be made for 'just intelligence' as it might for a 'just war', the two are not necessarily analogous because police intelligence-gathering takes place continuously and is not dependent on a declaration of hostilities or other clear statement of change in the *status quo*. Some have argued that ethical practice and intelligence work cannot ever be reconciled and that the best that the police can hope for is the establishment (and publication; transparency is vital) of a set of principles for resolving ethical problems as they emerge (see, for example Gill, 2009).

In July, 2014, the CoP established just such a set of principles in the form of its Code of Ethics for policing (CoP, 2014b). Every member of the policing profession in England and Wales is expected to uphold the principles of accountability, integrity, openness, fairness, leadership, respect, honesty, objectivity and selflessness. Based on the Nolan principles underpinning conduct in public life (CSPL, 1995), these principles seem relevant and appropriate to the work, but it is easy to see how tensions may arise in the intelligence milieu. Moreover, specialised groups in organisations create their own sets of behaviours, attitudes and values that shape their professional work ethos. The activities of the SDS provide an exemplar in the intelligence context. The simple existence of policies and procedures does not necessarily guarantee compliance. While the code represents a bold attempt to 'strengthen the existing procedures and regulations for ensuring standards of professional behaviour for both police officers and police staff' (CoP, 2014b, p.6), it is in the intelligence world it is likely to meet some of its most significant tests.

Summary

Arguably, concerns about the growth of the surveillance state and policing's capabilities in that context have been mitigated to some degree by the increasing openness of practitioners about the work even if it broadly is understood that complete transparency may be in the interests of no one, save the criminal element. Although the discrete methods and tactics used properly remain hidden, citizens have learned much about the work from the extensive reporting on relevant police activities, its regulation and the introduction of the oversight regime. Whether that is enough to address public concern is far from settled. The need for police intelligence work may be a pragmatic reality, but the institution needs to make a better case for it to a sceptical public. It also needs to develop and support its intelligence staff in much more effective ways. As this analysis shows, however, advocates of change face significant challenges in that regard, not the least of which is overcoming cultural bias against reflection and soft skills.

Notes

[1]   Article 8, European Convention on Human Rights.

[2]   See Clutterbuck (2002).

[3]   Prior to 1997, surveillance, informer and undercover deployments were guided by Home Office circulars and internal rules.

[4]   The commission was referring to the Baumber, Pearce and Ratcliffe reports (1975, 1978, and 1986 respectively).

[5]   Palmer refers to the spending of £6 billion on a failed attempt to introduce a new NHS data system and to a report by parliament's Intelligence and Security Committee on a similarly costly and unsuccessful attempt to introduce a computer system designed to enable government departments to consult secret intelligence.

[6]   A notable omission from that list is the facility to intercept communications, which remains the preserve of specialists investigating the most serious of crimes.

Further reading

Ball, K and Wood, DM (Eds.) (2006), *Report on the Surveillance Society for the Information Commissioner*. London: Surveillance Studies Network.

Grieve, J (2004), Lawfully audacious: a reflective journey, in C. Harfield, J. Grieve and A. MacVean (Eds.), *Handbook of Intelligent Policing: Consilience, Crime Control, and Community Safety*. Oxford: OUP, pp.13-24.

Waddington, PAJ (2005). Slippery slopes and civil libertarian pessimism. *Policing & Society*, 15 (3), p.353-75.

THREE

Organisational structures

Introduction

National security is no more the preserve of SIAs than preventing and detecting crime, particularly transnational organised crime, can be left to the police. The SIAs' missions are to: protect the nation and its interests against threats to national security (MI5); to gather intelligence outside of the UK in support of relevant government policies (MI6); and to maintain the safety and security of the nation's cyber connections and infrastructure (GCHQ). The police mission is to: protect life and property; maintain public order; prevent crime; and bring offenders to justice.

Those mission statements demonstrate the obvious overlaps between crime, terrorism and national security, and the need for state policies and practices that reflect that reality. The state needs an effective national security framework, one capable of supporting the relevant institutions in the ordinary course of their business but sufficiently flexible that it can operate at a higher tempo when needed (such as at times of national emergency). The UK's relationship with international and European policing bodies concerned in the fight against transnational organised crime, namely, Interpol, Europol, and the Supplementary Information Request (National Entry) Bureau (SIRENE) is also important, as are the national, regional and local arrangements for combating serious and organised crime, and terrorism.

Intelligence framework

It is difficult to conceive of any government duty greater than its responsibility to preserve the safety and security of its citizens. Although a case can be made for a permanent operational command and control centre, there already is an extensive network of agencies, centres and units (including the police and other law enforcement agencies) tasked with defending the realm and maintaining the safety and security of the UK's citizens. Since the 1970s, at times of regional or national emergency or whenever there is a threat to Britain's overseas interests, representatives of those bodies have been brought together in a committee chaired by a member of the executive. The actual constitution of the group depends on the nature of the event or threat, but it usually is chaired by the Prime Minister or, in their absence, by another government minister. This committee is known by the acronym COBR(A), the shortened form of Cabinet Briefing Room A, where meetings initially were held (a rather mundane explanation that does not merit the frisson of excitement that routinely accompanies news that a meeting is to be convened).

Parliamentary oversight of intelligence is provided by a statutory body, the Intelligence and Security Committee (ISC). The ISC oversees the work of the UK's intelligence apparatus. Oversight in that context extends beyond operations to the policies, logistics and budgets of MI5, MI6 and GCHQ; the central intelligence machinery made up of the National Security Council and its Secretariat, the Joint Intelligence Organisation, and the Joint Intelligence Committee; and the wider intelligence community that includes defence intelligence, the Office for Security and Counter-Terrorism (OSCT), the Joint Terrorism Analysis Centre, Foreign and Commonwealth Office research analyses, and of course all major policing bodies. The histories and operations of the SIAs already are well documented. The ISC publishes an annual report and the reports of various inquiries also are widely available.

OSCT

The OSCT acts as a bridge between the Home Office and policing. Established in 2007, the OSCT represented a significant expansion of the Home Office's role in coordinating the UK's counter-terrorism (CT) strategy, CONTEST. It is responsible for developing terrorism legislation and ensuring that, as far as possible, the UK is prepared for any terrorist attack within its borders or in any of its dependent territories on its critical infrastructure or against significant public figures. The OSCT also formulates CT policy, although the operational lead is taken by the Metropolitan Police Service (MPS). Day-to-day management of CT operations is overseen by the force's Counter Terrorism Command (CTC). The CONTEST strategy is separated into four programmes. Policing plays a leading role in each. They are:

- Prevent – prevent terrorist attacks by tackling radicalisation and the factors that contribute to it.
- Pursue – disrupt terrorists and their operations both in the UK and overseas.

- Protect – reduce the vulnerability of the UK and of its overseas interests to terrorist attack.
- Prepare – ensure the UK is as prepared as it can be for dealing with the consequences of a terrorist attack (Home Office, 2011b).

The programmes are meant to complement each other so that a broad front is maintained against the threat of terrorism. In practice, the social situation and the perceived level of threat at any given time will determine which of the strands has primacy.

This study suggests that CT officers believe that in CONTEST, the UK has the policies in place that it needs to counter the terrorist threat. The strategy was explained by a research respondent, a senior officer of the Police Service of Northern Ireland (PSNI), in the following terms. The state and its agencies aim to prevent terrorism in all its forms (Prevent). No liberal democracy can frustrate every terrorist act; therefore, the state needs the capacity to pursue those it cannot prevent engaging in terrorist activity (Pursue). The state needs sufficient resources to capture or neutralise everyone who wishes to do it harm; therefore, it needs situational and social crime prevention strategies capable of countering the malign intent of those beyond its reach (Protect). Finally, no matter how many obstacles are put in their way, terrorists (often by exploiting the very freedoms that citizens hold dear) invariably find a way to breach the state's defences. Therefore, in the aftermath of any attack, the state needs its emergency and other public services to be capable of responding speedily and effectively (Prepare).

Clearly, intelligence work is vital to the success of each of these initiatives. Intelligence informs annual reviews of each programme and the wider strategy (now in its third iteration). Since 2011, the Home Office has reported annually on CONTEST. The strategy is interesting in its own right, but it also is notable that its perceived success persuaded the Home Office to adapt it for inclusion in its first National Strategic Assessment of Serious and Organised Crime (Home Office, 2013). This new version also provides the conceptual model for the NCA. Having set that scene, the focus of this chapter from here on largely is on the policing structures that complement those national security arrangements.

The international dimension

In the past, few UK law enforcement personnel outside of the specialist detective squads and ports staff have needed to know much about international policing arrangements. With the benefit of hindsight, it can now be seen that the requirement for effective transnational policing arrangements grew most quickly during a generation in which the Home Office and a significant section of the police elite were investing practically and intellectually in policies better characterised by localism (such as various iterations of the neighbourhood policing programme). In the 21st century, the negative effects of globalisation, and the exponential increases in people trafficking, smuggling and transnational organised crime more generally, require officers (effectively) to police a global village. Greater awareness of the international dimension of crime has become essential rather than optional. Three bodies are particularly significant: Interpol; Europol; and SIRENE.

Interpol

Founded in 1923 and more formally known as the International Criminal Police Organisation, Interpol is the largest and oldest international police organisation in the world. It is an intergovernmental institution, with a membership of 190 countries. Interpol has no operational involvement in investigations, but provides four basic services to member nations. First, authorised law enforcement agencies and strategic partners (including, for example, the World Customs Organisation) can share information around the clock via a secure global police information and support system, which connects all 190 National Central Bureaus (NCBs). Second, Interpol maintains numerous databases that may be accessed by member countries. These include extensive collections of images, fingerprints, stolen passports and DNA profiles (though few countries have contributed as many profiles to that database as the UK). Third, it sets international standards and offers certification and accreditation in policing and security subjects. It also supports law enforcement agencies to address new forms of crimes, develop research partnerships, and in post-conflict or priority areas (through, for example, the Operational Assistance, Services, and Infrastructure initiative, to build capacity to combat those new crimes by delivering training in cybercrime and digital forensics for instance. Finally, Interpol provides 24/7 support for police operations including emergency and crisis response (Interpol, 2013). These usually are managed through the NCBs. The UK's NCB is part of the NCA and is based in Manchester in the latter's International Crime Bureau.

Europol

An intelligence agency capable of exchanging and analysing information affecting at least two member states (MS) was agreed in principle in 1992. The Europol Drugs Unit became operational in 1994 and continued until 1999 when it was replaced by Europol, which was funded by MS. In 2010, Europol was given EU agency status and now is considered to be the law enforcement agency of the European Union. It has been argued that its switch to agency status was significant because it gave the European Parliament budgetary authority over the agency and 'indirect influence' over its direction (Occhipinti, 2015, p.237).

Europol's HQ in the Netherlands has around 900 staff working with the law enforcement agencies of the 28 MS and with other partners including Australia, Canada, the US and Norway (Europol, 2015). Europol styles itself as 'a support centre for law enforcement operations, a hub for criminal information, and a centre for law enforcement expertise' (Europol, 2015, p.1). About 20% of its staff members are European Liaison Officers (ELOs) seconded from MS. They work in the Liaison Bureau at Europol HQ. In 2008, the UK had eight staff in the bureau representing the Serious Organised Crime Agency (SOCA), the MPS, HMRC and the Scottish Crime and Drugs Enforcement Agency. Today, the UK's Europol National Unit (ENU) also is situated in the NCA's International Crime Bureau. A similar number of UK officers are currently deployed. They work with ELOs from other states but also represent UK interests in accordance with UK law.

Unlike Interpol, although agency staff do not have police powers, they do take part in operations in EU countries. Usually, that is in company with local officers as part of a joint investigation team. On average, Europol deals with more than 18,000 cases each year. Its priorities are international criminal and terrorist groups, but it also claims expertise in combating drug trafficking, illicit immigration, human trafficking, illicit vehicle trafficking, cybercrime, money laundering and counterfeiting (Europol, 2015). Europol's 'competence' covers terrorism and other forms of serious crime affecting 'two or more MS ... in such a way as to require a common approach by the MS owing to the scale, significance and consequences of the offences' (EU, 2009, p.L121.39).

Like Interpol, it provides 24/7 support for law enforcement operations involving MS and manages databases that can be accessed by those agencies via their national units. Progress towards establishing a comprehensive and credible central information repository, in the shape of the Europol Information System (EIS), has however been much slower than its architects hoped. In 2008, a wider review of Europol found that the EIS was under-used and contained data that was of poor quality (HLEUC, 2008). The agency also maintains an Analytical Work Files database, which contains files on the work in progress of the agency, either in regard to specific operations or to particular initiatives (such as human trafficking).

The agency's Terrorism Situation and Trend Report (Te-Sat) and Serious and Organized Crime Threat Assessment (SOCTA) have been described as Europol's 'most important intelligence products' (Ballaschk, 2015, p.37), although one of the research respondents, a Europol analyst, said that both rely in large part on information over which the agency has little meaningful control. MS and other parties are not bound to submit data to Europol in any particular format. Submissions are of variable quality and length. Some are timely and comprehensive; others include only minimal relevant detail. Europol's task of combining, comparing or contrasting data from different submissions can be challenging endeavours, requiring more of a broad-brush approach than some might consider appropriate for such putatively important documents.

While the challenges of completing the Te-Sat and SOCTA previously have received little scholarly attention, other shortcomings have been noted. For example, in 2008, Europol's contribution to sharing intelligence about terrorism was found to be insignificant (Bures, 2008). In the same year, the House of Lords European Union Committee (HLEUC, 2008) questioned its ability to fulfil its mandate of providing a hub for criminal information. The committee felt that it was of particular concern that four fifths of the information exchanged by national liaison officers stationed at Europol is exchanged without actually going through Europol, which it considered the 'antithesis of the purpose of Europol' (HLEUC, 2008, p.8).

Bures and HLEUC, separately, concluded that the most significant factor in that context was MS' unwillingness to trust other states with sensitive information (Bures, 2008; HLEUC, 2008). In her evidence to the inquiry, Den Boer argued that 'As long as MS keep the intelligence to themselves [the success of Europol] just will not happen, so the culture of change will have to take place there rather than within Europol itself' (cited in HLEUC, 2008, p.23). The committee did not believe that meaningful change could be achieved. MS favoured their pre-existing, informal, intelligence-sharing arrangements over the officially sanctioned channels. There was little appetite in MS' law enforcement agencies to relinquish ownership of information (even less in the context of terrorism – see Den Boer, 2015). Police culture too was a significant issue; Europol was seen by police professionals as having been imposed on them by EU politicians. There was only a grudging acceptance of it and no desire to abandon often long-standing bilateral arrangements in which professionals had confidence (Bures, 2008). Those kinds of arrangements benefit individual MS, but they do not contribute to wider knowledge and understanding of threat and risk across the European Community. Of course, as one researcher has highlighted, this by-passing of Europol protocols also raises questions about the extent to which personal data receives the protection that it merits under EU law (Ballaschk, 2015).

Both Bures' study and the House of Lords' inquiry predate Europol's switch to agency status, so it is reasonable to assess the extent to which the adjustment affected its relationship with MS' law enforcement agencies, namely, whether there are any signs that those cultural barriers have been broken down. The scholarly research into the work of the agency post-2010 suggests not. Safjański, a senior Polish police officer and formerly a Europol insider, notes the resilience of police culture, identifying a process he terms 'direct action', the same tendency to use the Liaison Bureau to bypass the Europol central function identified five years earlier (2013, p.57). He argues that even though MS support the agency in principle 'they lack a common vision … [which] has consequences for the development of its operational capacity' (Safjański, 2013, p.57).

It is generally accepted that the bulk of intelligence passing between ENUs and Europol is managed by their bureau officers without finding its way into the EIS. Moreover, the strategic assessments submitted to Europol by MS are not always as comprehensive as they might be. Applying the principle of 'garbage in, garbage out' to those processes, there is cause to question the credibility of the EIS as the agency's institutional memory and the value of the strategic and tactical intelligence reports Europol produces reciprocally for MS. While it is axiomatic that an intelligence picture is always partial and confused, it is something of a stretch to expect analysts to make sense of it in these circumstances. Without that 'missing' intelligence, those analyses are bound to have limited value. Safjański set out a number of options for change, but, given the reactionary forces he describes, it is difficult to argue with his assertion that without a fundamental shift in the relationship between Europol and MS' law enforcement agencies the issue will always undermine the agency's operational effectiveness.

It has been argued that the change should be understood as confirmation of a broader shift towards supranationalism in the EU's institutions (Occhipinti, 2015). That is a perfectly rational interpretation of events; supranationalist institutions will be an inevitable by-product of the political union that the EU Commission seeks. Even if that goal is eventually achieved, Bures and Safjanski's research suggests that MS' appetite for real change in Europol is much less than some would have us believe. If the discourses and policy decisions that are now coming forward within the EU are to be interpreted as signs of a slow drift towards supranational police cooperation, that argument should carry a caveat. Europol's history suggests that even that development fundamentally will not change the way that MS' law enforcement agencies share information with each other and with the agency. There are too many concerns about Europol's direction of travel. As far back as 2006, a rather prescient warning was given that there was an insufficiently meaningful debate about the role of the agency, and that its seemingly inexhaustible appetite for increased power was justified by neither political will nor operational demand from the MS (Hayes, 2006, p.9). Some nine years on, that appetite shows no sign of diminishing. Unlike Interpol, whose remit is little changed even if technology has enabled it to extend its reach, there are significant concerns about Europol's mission creep and the EU's future plans for it, which, as Occhipinti has argued, are bound up with its desire for supranational institutions that allow it to assume the political and financial control of institutions that currently are controlled by MS.

SIRENE and SIS II

SIRENE is the network that supports cooperation and coordination between law enforcement agencies in MS. Its use is overseen by the European Data Protection Supervisor, but its security is the responsibility of the EU Agency for large-scale IT systems (eu-LISA). SIRENE provides the gateway to, the human interface with, Schengen Information System (SIS). Currently, bureau officials have exclusive access to the system that now in its second iteration is more commonly known as SIS II, which is a collection of databases used by law enforcement agencies and border staff to check for fugitives, missing persons, lost/stolen travel documents and stolen motor vehicles. At international transit points, officials can scan identity documents, transmit them securely via secure network and have them checked almost instantaneously.

The UK's NCA hosts the UK SIRENE Bureau and is also the UK central authority for European arrest warrants. Even though the UK has opted out of many of the Schengen arrangements, it has opted in to SIS II. Therefore, UK police, customs officers and UKBF staff can communicate directly with the SIRENE Bureau via the Police National Computer. Plans are at an advanced stage for access to be extended to all UK police forces, including Police Scotland and the PSNI (CoP, 2015c). There are a number of options available to officers who wish to make use of the system. In the context of this analysis, the most significant is the opportunity in criminal investigations to place an alert on a person, vehicle or container requesting that a discreet check is made (without disclosing the existence of the alert) if they are located. The information that may be collected in that check might include the place, date, time seen; type of vehicle; points of departure and arrival; route taken; travelling companions; details of property being carried; and so on (CoP, 2015c). The utility of SIS II to law enforcement agencies attempting to track suspects or shipments of illicit cargo through Europe may be inferred, but it is difficult for outsiders to assess the real value of SIS II or the extent to which its use may represent a breach of basic rights and liberties. A report on its operation is produced annually and is available online, but, packed with jargon and obfuscation, it offers little of real value to the lay reader (see, for example, eu-LISA, 2014).

The national dimension

The most significant efforts to restructure the police intelligence apparatus in recent years have been the post-Bichard development of the Police National Database (PND) and the Home Office's launch of the coalition government's *Serious and Organised Crime Strategy* (Home Office, 2014b). Introduced in 2011, PND removed some of the barriers to sharing information between forces. PND software converts disparate data recording methods into a format that can be shared across forces. Data from local databases is automatically uploaded to the PND. Important in its own right, the strategy also signalled the introduction of the NCA and the Government Agency Intelligence Network (GAIN) and a further strengthening of regional policing and intelligence arrangements. These are by no means the only units managing intelligence at the national or regional levels. For example, the City of London Police's National Fraud Intelligence Bureau (NFIB) plays a significant role in identifying serial fraudsters and the involvement of criminal networks in fraud by analysing many millions of frauds reported to it by individuals, business, and the wider commercial banking, insurance and telecommunications sectors. The merits of the NFIB or bodies like it are not underestimated; they are worthy of scholarly research but word limits and a selfish need for narrative clarity mean that analyses of sector-specific initiatives are not included here.

Another development worthy of note is the expansion of the confidential intelligence unit (CIU) system. CIUs have existed for many years in national police agencies and larger forces, but recently have become a more significant feature of the national architecture. Their purpose is to connect force intelligence systems with the NCA, counter-terrorism units and police agencies overseas, and manage the most sensitive sources of intelligence available to the police. CIUs act as firewalls, separating out the information from the source (through processes known as sanitisation and grading – see Chapter Five) before disseminating it in accordance with Government Security Classification (GSC) requirements.

National Crime Agency (NCA)

In 2013, the coalition government replaced the short-lived (and largely unlamented) SOCA with NCA. The NCA also took over the MPS Child Exploitation and Online Protection Centre as an individual command and also assumed some of the responsibilities of the UK Border Agency and of NPIA. Arguably, SOCA's problems were not solely presentational. Few empirical studies of its short life have been carried out. One that compared publicly available data on SOCA with that of one of its predecessor agencies, the National Crime Squad (NCS), found that in terms of number of operations to seizures of drugs and the recovery of assets, SOCA's performance was relatively poor (Sproat, 2011). In a second study, the same author argued that there was a 'staggeringly large discrepancy between the official description of the nature and extent of organised crime and SOCA's use of the traditional and new tools for policing the problem' (Sproat, 2011, p.346). Sproat found that despite the claims made by the Home Office for SOCA, in an average year it 'convicted just over one percent of the people said to be involved in [organised crime] in the UK outwith Scotland' (2011, p.347). On first reading, that seems very low, but the inability to compare like for like data or to be able to measure the impact of the conviction of that one percent should give pause for further reflection on its true meaning.

Opinions differ on the reasons for the abolition of SOCA and the creation of the NCA, which took over the former's responsibilities, employs many of its staff and in many ways looks a lot like the body it replaced. Certainly, the NCA has a wider remit, including greater powers than the agency it replaced, and the desire for a more robust and capable replacement may have been a factor. The appointment of a senior police chief as its first head also signalled a clear break with the recent past. The decision to employ a former spymaster as SOCA's head cast the die very early on for the way in which the organisation would present itself to, and be perceived by, the public and partners. The new chief argued that, lacking the leadership role that is part of the NCA's mandate, SOCA 'operated in an environment where the end to end response was therefore not always coordinated effectively' (Bristow, 2015, p.2), which some may interpret as an admission that SOCA lacked the ability (or perhaps the authority it needed) to carry through its plans. In its first 18 months, the NCA has been much more visible than its predecessor, a deliberate strategy intended to counter the 'what has the agency ever done for us?' type questions that were consistently levelled at the unnecessarily (and ultimately self-defeatingly) secretive SOCA.

The new chief announced that the NCA was sharing its specialist capabilities (for example in relation to kidnap offences) and also was in receipt of specialist support from the UK SIAs (Bristow, 2015). Furthermore, the agency has claimed that it will be 'more visible to the public than SOCA and will operate with a culture of openness and transparency' (PSA, 2013). The new agency is a non-ministerial government department with a strength of around 4,500 officers. Reflecting its diverse antecedents, NCA officers may carry the powers of a constable, a customs officer, an immigration officer, or any combination of these. The NCA's mission is to tackle serious and organised crime; strengthen the UK's borders; fight fraud and cybercrime; and protect children and young people from sexual abuse and exploitation. The NCA also plays an extremely important role in international and transnational policing and effectively is the gateway to European and other international law enforcement agencies for British policing. Its strategy is modelled on the CONTEST '4Ps' strategy. In this case, the acronym stands for:

- Prevent – stopping people from engaging in serious and organised crime.
- Pursue – prosecuting and disrupting people engaged in serious and organised criminality.
- Protect – increasing protection against serious and organised crime.
- Prepare – reducing the impact of this criminality where it takes place.

The agency's director-general has the statutory authority to direct police forces to assist the NCA. Early indications are that the power will be used sparingly, if at all. The agency seems to favour partnership with other policing bodies and that is a policy it consistently espouses. Recent developments include an enhanced partnership agreement with Police Scotland, the broadening of its collaboration with the MPS in the development of the Middle Market Drugs Partnership into the Organised Crime Partnership and a new joint NCA/GCHQ unit combining GCHQ's technical skills with the NCA's investigatory expertise to combat child sexual exploitation and cybercrime.

The agency operates a central, multi-agency intelligence hub, which analyses intelligence generated both by the agency and by its partners to provide a national picture of crime threats and crime trends. Unlike SOCA, the NCA states that it is committed to working to NIM principles. It follows that, once generated, that picture should drive the NCA's strategic intelligence collection and longer-term operational activities. It also should inform operational activity through the new national coordination and tasking group (NCAT), a crucially important element in planned policing, and key to NIM, that has for so long been missing from the putatively pyramidal structure of ILP in the UK. NCAT's role is to coordinate, prioritise and target NCA activity against serious and organised crime.

The agency was bound to face challenges as it bedded in. It inherited from SOCA an ageing workforce with a high proportion of officers at supervisory levels, and staff morale and motivation was not all that it could have been: the 2013 NCA staff survey revealed that only 55% of NCA staff were proud to tell others that they were employed by the agency; just 39% would recommend it as a place to work; and only 40% felt motivated to do their best (NCARRB, 2014). In February 2015, it was criticised by the House of Commons Home Affairs Committee for seizing only £22.5m of criminals' assets in its first year and was warned that it needed to make 'drastic improvements' in that aspect of its work (Travis, 2015). It recently was reported that the NCA's chief and six other executives would leave the agency prematurely. The NCA has denied that their departures and the earlier reports are connected (Beckford, 2015). The agency's ambition is that the public trust it and criminals fear it (NCA, nd). On this evidence it may be some time before either goal is achieved.

Police Counter Terrorism Network (PCTN)

The PCTN is made up of the MPS Counter Terrorism Command (CTC) and eight regional counter-terrorism hubs (RCTUs) located in the police areas of Avon and Somerset, Hertfordshire, Greater Manchester, Nottinghamshire, South Wales, Thames Valley, West Midlands and West Yorkshire. Given its historic role in countering terrorism, its close relationship with the Home Office and the security agencies, and its physical presence in the capital, it is unsurprising that CTC leads in this field. The joint aim of the units is to deliver a coordinated response to terrorism; provide expertise and support to police forces, local authorities and business in their designated areas; and supplement the security agencies' efforts against terrorism when the need arises.

Regional organised crime units (ROCUs)

With the aims of increasing the police's ability to tackle the threat of organised crime across England and Wales and to provide a specialist policing capability to local forces, 10 ROCUs have been established across the UK. The mission of each unit is simple: to tackle organised crime groups causing the greatest level of harm to communities. Each ROCU is configured slightly differently, but as a rule they bring together specialised teams and functions to form a single structure. These may include investigation units; asset recovery units; protected persons units; covert and technical surveillance units; intelligence units; and operational security units. Also embedded within ROCUs are representatives of GAIN, HMRC, UKBF and, not least, NCA staff.

GAIN

GAIN's primary role is to channel intelligence to public sector and other partners, such as the National Trading Standards Board and the Gangmasters Licencing Authority, and to ensure that relevant information from those bodies is passed to the ROCUs in timely and useful ways. The presence of a GAIN coordinator in each of the ROCUs is intended to enhance the regional capacity to combat serious and organised crime. Their role is to ensure that crime-related knowledge held within one government agency that may be of value to another is passed to others in a timely and useful fashion. Data still must be shared in lawful and ethical ways that comply with relevant law and regulation so that it can be used by the ROCU or other

GAIN partner to prevent/disrupt criminal activity and/or seize the proceeds of crime.

Police forces

Given the level of debate about force amalgamation and regionalisation in recent years, it may come as a surprise to some that there still are 43 separate Home Office-controlled police forces in England and Wales. Forces vary considerably in size, capability and capacity. The City of London Police numbers around 1,000 officers, while the MPS has more than 33,000. Provincial forces largely have somewhere between 1,200 and 4,000 officers, and major conurbations many more (for example Greater Manchester Police and the West Midlands force, which polices the Metropolitan county of the West Midlands, each have around 8,000 officers).

Almost all forces have a headquarters intelligence unit, usually described as a force intelligence bureau (FIB), which collates and evaluates information using intelligence cycle principles (discussed earlier). Ideally, the work conducted by the bureau should support strategic priorities identified through NIM strategic and tasking processes (discussed later), but it also is the 'hub of all information, tip-offs and rumours about criminal activity' (Cheshire Constabulary, nd). At this operating level, seeing the wood for the trees is greatly complicated by what Sheptycki (2004) termed 'noise'. Partly, that is a product of unfocused collection (also discussed later), but also too often intelligence reports have been used as performance indicators and that can completely skew the collection effort. As the term suggests, noise can distract intelligence staff and scarce resources may be dissipated. FIBs usually contain a mix of police officers and staff performing a variety of roles such as researcher, analyst or intelligence officer. They process the information that comes in from members of the public, other police forces and law enforcement agencies or from elsewhere in the force (such as that collected in the ordinary course of police business). Intelligence officers perform an extremely important task termed 'sanitisation', the cleaning of any trace of the identity of the person, group or organisation that provided it. They are responsible too for assigning an initial indicator of value to each piece of information received.

Depending on the size and capability of the force, surveillance or other covert policing functions also may be attached. Those kinds of teams have been called the 'operational arm' of the bureau (West Midlands Police Authority, 2012, p.2). The largest forces may have teams of undercover officers, test purchase officers and a technical intelligence collection capability (that might include open source research, telephony and computer analysis). Often, less well-resourced forces establish agreements with their larger neighbours to gain access to those resources. In most forces, CHISs are managed by DSUs but currently DSUs are being reduced in number to deliver economies of scale and to divert resources to policing's front line. On one level, that is perfectly understandable in an era of austerity, but it suggests that commanders are not as persuaded of the merits of ILP as they once were. It also raises questions about commanders' conceptions of crime and the continuing identification of frontline policing with 'the mean streets' and little else.

The final element in the intelligence pyramid is its foundation, that is, the intelligence offices based in LPUs in each force. Forces do at least have in place uniform structures and processes that, in principle, can facilitate cross-flows of intelligence and support the kind of inter-operability that often is needed to address modern-day social problems. However, the real commitment of the organisation to those mechanisms remains moot; in this age of austerity, the signs are that they too have been identified as back-office functions by commanders and therefore are ripe for cuts.

UK serious and organised crime strategy

Launched at the same time as NCA and GAIN, the Home Office's serious and organised crime strategy attempts to draw on lessons learned from previous work to counter-terrorism (Home Office, 2013). Conceptually, the strategy underpins the work of NCA, ROCUs and some of the UK's police forces (Home Office, 2014b). In much the same way as the CONTEST strategy, it seeks to encourage the adoption of a range of tactics to reduce threats and vulnerabilities in a holistic way rather than, for example, focusing on arrest and seizure figures that often do not reflect impact or outcomes.

Summary

The UK national intelligence architecture is made up of a network of institutions, including the armed forces, the SIAs and the police. In principle, they work symbiotically to protect the nation and its interests. The UK is a member of Interpol and Europol and also subscribes to SIRENE and SIS II. Official assessment of Europol's value to the UK is difficult because of the existence of cultural barriers to formal information sharing. There are concerns in some MS about Europol's mission creep and also about the EU's future plans for the agency. The national framework is claimed to be more robust for the addition of new regional units, which have filled the vacuum that existed between police forces and the national agencies, but as yet it is too early to make any meaningful assessment of their value. Developments in police forces, notably the reductions in number and size of DSUs, smack of short-termism and are rather less welcome. Further analysis of the longer-term ramifications of those changes might also include some reflection on what is meant, in the modern era, by the notoriously mutable term 'front line'.

Further reading

College of Policing (2015): *Governance* [Internet]. https://www.app.college.police.uk/app-content/intelligence-management/governance/

Harfield, C; Harfield, K (2008), *Intelligence, Investigation, Community and Partnership*. Oxford: OUP.

James, A (2013), *Examining intelligence-led policing*. Basingstoke: Palgrave MacMillan.

FOUR

The legal and procedural framework

Introduction

This chapter assesses the rules underpinning lawful intelligence practice in the UK.[1] Law is but one element of a fragmented, intricate and convoluted legislative and oversight framework. The European Court of Human Rights (ECtHR) has been a significant driver of legislative and procedural change in this context. Certainly, its decisions spurred (one might argue, forced) the Home Office to construct the existing framework. Initially, what emerged was relatively fragile, a structure erected simply as a way of legitimising some covert activities the police had long undertaken but largely ignoring others. Over time, those other activities were brought within that structure, which was reinforced with more legislation, scrutiny in the form of parliamentary and statutory oversight, codes of practice and extended rights of redress. Undoubtedly, these have influenced intelligence practice, although for many, even these developments do not go far enough in securing its legitimacy.

Secret policing and human rights

A powerful argument can be made for secrecy; often it is essential to the success of intelligence work. Operational security is always an important element in intelligence and it is understandable that the police should prioritise it. Largely, the police have successfully hidden their intelligence-gathering capabilities. That ability to deflect scrutiny has relied on a kind of cultural hegemony, a tacit acceptance by the UK's establishment of the need for covert policing methods, no matter how underhand some of them may appear. That makes the process of unpicking the strands of the debate to explain how the police were able to keep their methods secret for so long rather challenging. Certainly, a significant factor was the legislative vacuum, which in turn meant only limited meaningful judicial scrutiny of the work.[2]

Regardless of the rhetoric from police commanders about operational independence, all policing is political.[3] Whether all law is politics essentially is a philosophical question, but certainly there are many who argue that politics occupies the space, the middle ground, between natural law and legal positivism, and can help to reconcile the two (see, for example, Vinx, 2007). That reasoning can explain how secret intelligence work continued to avoid real scrutiny for so long; there simply was neither sufficient political nor popular will to challenge it. Of course achieving a consensus is one thing; maintaining it is quite another. It was only a question of time until the political wind would change and cracks would begin to appear. At the end of the 20th century as daily life in the UK was remade in so many different ways in the information age, the politicisation of the law and order debate, declining deference in British society and an intensifying focus on individual liberties and human rights (particularly on the twin totems of privacy and fairness as expressed in the European Convention on Human Rights [ECHR]) by a resurgent Labour Party, first in opposition and then as the party of government, *inter alia* made the service's position untenable.[4]

Lifting the curtain

Earlier, it was noted that throughout most of its history the police service's unwavering commitment to secrecy masked the development of its intelligence apparatus. There was little appetite within policing to change the status quo, but, as so often is the case, one seemingly insignificant event (in this instance, the prosecution of an antique dealer for handling stolen goods) was the catalyst for fundamental institutional change. ECtHR is responsible for implementing the ECHR. The court's ruling in the case of *Malone vs the United Kingdom* ([1984] 7 EHRR 14) was the driver for the introduction of the Interception of Communications Act 1985 (IOCA). Arguably, IOCA was the first piece of legislation to address surveillance activity and the first legislative instrument of any kind to have a meaningful impact on police intelligence work.[5] The Act and its legacy can only properly be understood in the context of the ongoing debate over human rights and the balance of power between the state and the citizen.

In the modern era, the concepts of surveillance, privacy and data protection often are intertwined. The Data Protection Act 1998 (DPA) provisions are used extensively by intelligence officers as a means of indemnifying data controllers (who otherwise are under a statutory duty *inter alia* to maintain the confidentiality of personal data) to permit access to personal data (the Act refers to this as processing data) if the conditions specified in Section 29(1) DPA are met.[6] Personal data includes anything that may identify an individual. That includes telephone numbers, vehicle registrations and digital data (such as images of the individual, their home and so on). Data controllers are indemnified if the data is to be processed in connection with the prevention or detection of crime, the apprehension or prosecution of offenders, or the assessment or collection of any tax or duty or of any imposition of a similar nature. The exemption ends with the investigation meaning that post-hoc access requests always will be refused.[7]

DPA is a double-edged sword. An individual has the statutory right of subject access: the right to identify if their personal information has been processed by anyone. Public authorities are bound to have arrangements in place that recognise citizens' rights and that facilitate access. However, data processed under the Section 29(1) exemption is itself exempt from subject access. Routinely associated with DPA is the Freedom of Information Act 2000 (FOIA). The latter gives any person anywhere in the world, (subject to certain exemptions) the right to access information held by the UK's public authorities. The FOIA obliges public authorities to confirm or deny whether they hold the requested information and to communicate that information to the person seeking access. A variety of exemptions from disclosure are found under Sections 30 and 31 of the Act. Essentially, the police must comply with an FOIA request unless it is clear that prejudice would, or would be likely to, arise and it would not be in the public interest to disclose the information. The nature, degree and likelihood of the prejudice are factors that must be taken into account. Information also may be released through a publication scheme. In that case, the authority usually determines at policy level what should, and should not, be published. It is this last provision that has been the driver of so much online publishing activity by police forces and other law enforcement agencies in the past 15 years. The wealth of material that can now be found online is a direct result of FOIA.

Human rights

Though condemned by critics as little more than a criminals' charter, the Human Rights Act 1998 (HRA) and the debate that preceded its implementation were significant factors in the contemporary development of intelligence work and of UK policing more generally. The roots of that dialectic can be found in a broad-based international political movement that emerged in response to the crimes against humanity committed during the Second World War, but its rapid development in Britain in the 1990s was as much a product of party politics as anything else.[8] In opposition, Labour's support for a bill of rights was consistent with its credo even if individual liberties historically had not been a major focus for the party. Certainly, it seemed to strike a chord with the electorate and its plans also gave Labour a stick with which to beat the incumbent Conservative administration, which found itself cast as the enemy of freedom and eventually to perceived by many as irredeemably illiberal and reactionary, labels that also were firmly attached to policing in this period.

A pledge to enact legislation to secure citizens' rights was included in Labour's manifesto and when the party was elected to power in 1997, delivering on that promise became a priority. HRA was entered into the statute book the following year. The Act applies to all public authorities in the UK.[9] It requires UK courts and tribunals to interpret legislation so far as possible in a way compatible with the rights laid down in ECHR and it provides a remedy in UK courts for any breach of a Convention right. Since its implementation, the Act frequently has been cited as the cause of injustices (often in relation to a failure to deport a foreign criminal),[10] and its perceived shortcomings have been relentlessly exposed in the media.

In opposition, the Conservative Party, probably the Act's greatest critic, pledged to abolish HRA when it returned to power and indeed it seems intent on carrying through on that promise. Its plans include replacement of HRA with a British bill of rights and curtailment of the role of ECtHR. Confusingly, and perhaps counterintuitively given Conservative rhetoric, it has stated its intention to write the Convention into primary legislation. One can only speculate on how the government will meet its Convention obligations under the new arrangements if it is able to get them through parliament – by no means a certainty. It is worth noting that by 2014, ECtHR had decided on 1,652 cases concerning the UK; for all the rhetoric about the disproportionate impact of the court, more than 98% of cases were declared inadmissible or struck out (Gani, 2014). That perhaps puts into better perspective the real influences of ECtHR and the Convention on British jurisprudence.

Those principles have had a significant impact on policing practice in the modern era. It is claimed that they 'underpin every area of police work' and that all officers have been trained to understand that 'human rights must sit at the heart of the conception, planning, implementation and control of every aspect of the police operations' (CoP, 2015b, p.1).

In intelligence work, they are an essential element in tactical planning. Usually, situation-specific analyses are carried out during the planning process using the PLAN mnemonic (Figure 4.1), a heuristic device that ensures that proper consideration of human rights principles through to the conclusion of the operation and beyond.

Figure 4.1: The PLAN mnemonic

P – Proportionality: the advice most often associated with the concept is 'Do not use a sledgehammer to crack a nut'; one must balance the scale and scope of the proposed activity against the gravity and extent of perceived offence. The action should cause the least possible intrusion into the private life of the subject and others. The action is an appropriate use of the legislation and all reasonable alternatives have been considered. The application should record why those alternatives were not implemented.

L – Legality: the action must be lawful according to statute, other legislation, or legal precedent; internal rules or guidelines do not pass the legality test (as Malone, Govell, Khan and Halford show).

A – Accountability: relevant decisions and actions must be justified and recorded and that applies also to decisions not to act (best practice dictates that decision logs or policy books should be maintained for each operation).

N – Necessity: human rights infringements (such as collateral intrusion) must always be justified. Intelligence staff must be able to demonstrate that the proposed action is necessary to achieve a positive outcome to the operation; identifying a suspect's address is something that often can be achieved by scanning public records rather than by deploying a surveillance team or CHIS even if they are readily available for deployment.

European Convention on Human Rights

Privacy is a right protected in law for all European citizens. In fact, it is but one of 17 key rights and freedoms secured by ECHR; these are set out in Section 1, Articles 1–18 of the Convention. In the context of intelligence work and covert policing, perhaps the most significant are Article 2 (right to life), Article 5 (right to liberty and security), Article 6 (right to a fair trial), Article 8 (the aforementioned right to privacy) and Article 13 (right to an effective remedy before national authorities for ECHR violations). Many judicial proceedings have had a bearing on intelligence work, but a relatively small number of rulings are key to understanding how that work is regulated today. *Malone* is one of those cases. Others include *Osman, Preston, Govell, Khan* and *Halford*.

Osman vs the UK (29 EHRR 245 [28 October 1998]) is one of the leading human rights cases involving the UK. The tragic circumstances are that a teacher's obsession with a 15-year-old former pupil eventually led him to assault the boy and to kill the boy's father. It soon became obvious that the police had not recognised the danger soon enough, even though they had information that might have allowed them to prevent the attacks or at least offer protection to the family. That complaint of police negligence was not upheld by the UK courts, but the complainant took the case to ECtHR. The court determined that there had been a violation of Article 6 ECHR because the domestic case had been struck out (quite properly on the basis of UK law) and therefore there had not been a full trial on the facts as the Convention required. The case turned on the UK's blanket ban on claims of negligence in this context. The court held that such a ban was unlawful and should be overturned. *Osman* had a significant impact on policing and intelligence practice because of its impact in negligence cases against the police. The case brought home to the police the need to warn an intended victim when there was any threat or risk against them.[11]

Generally when someone is considered to be in real and immediate danger, a warning – known to the police (for obvious reasons) as an *Osman* or 'threat to life' warning – should be given. The police also may offer protective measures, but it is up to the intended victim to take any action they deem appropriate. As was highlighted earlier, the police have moral, ethical and legal duties of care to informers. From the outset, they must consider their informers' safety and welfare during and after their deployment ends. In reality, intelligence staffs regularly identify such threats – hardly surprising given that much of their attention is focused on organised crime and that informers are vital to their success. Offenders rarely seek legal remedies when illicit business goes awry and all too often situations arise that require intelligence staff to take, or at least consider, action. Intervening too early can have implications for operations and for operational security; too late may result in harm to individuals and/or communities, reputational and financial damage to the intelligence force or agency, and diminished faith in the policing institution.

Interception of Communications Act 1985

The British state's ability to intercept citizens' communications is well understood, but the origin of its right to conduct that activity is 'obscure' (Birkett, 1957, p.1). Certainly, it has been exercised for many years. On the establishment of a regular post office in 1657, 'it was stated in the Ordinance to be the best Means to discover and prevent any dangerous and wicked Designs against the Commonwealth', but the activity probably pre-dates even that event (Birkett, 1957, p.1). Interception has always been controversial and 'the subject of public agitation from time to time' (Birkett, 1957, p.1). That has been no less true in the modern era. A turning point was reached following the unsuccessful prosecution of James Malone, an antique dealer charged with the dishonest handling of stolen goods. During the proceedings, it was disclosed that the officer in charge of the case, in contravention of the Home Office guidelines, had in his notebook a written record of one of Malone's telephone conversations. In confirming that interception had taken place, the officer's note revealed what should have remained secret. Even though in all other regards relevant guidelines had been followed properly, Malone sued the police on the grounds that the monitoring and recording of his conversations without his consent was unlawful.

Eventually, in 1984, the case arrived at ECtHR.[12] Its decision turned on the UK's arrangements for intercepting citizens' communications, which, in the court's view, did not provide the minimum degree of legal protection to which citizens were entitled because they were not supported by legislation or by legal precedent. Mindful of its implications for other police investigations and for the continuing utility of the interception tactic, the government moved quickly (though as many have recognised, without much enthusiasm) to legislate; IOCA came into operation in April 1986. The Act was not intended to control every form of surveillance; there was little enough of an appetite in government for that, but the specificity of its objectives (largely limited to ensuring that the UK complied with *Malone*) meant that its reaction to the court's finding received only a lukewarm welcome. *The Times* described it as a 'dumb insolence measure ... in which the minimum action possible is grudgingly taken to comply with the letter of rulings under international agreements' (cited in Spencer, 2009, p.374). Civil libertarians criticised it for, once again, privileging the state over the individual. In response to the Bill that preceded it, the *Financial Times* observed that 'at every sensitive point of balance between the rights of the individual and the interests of the state, it fails the individual' (cited in Lloyd, 1986, p.95). Jurists meanwhile criticised it as bad law, which (for example) promised more than it delivered (Lloyd, 1986) or represented 'a largely procedural rather than substantive reform' (Fenwick, 2000, p.346).

That is not to downplay the significance of IOCA for the policing institution. The Act, and the debate surrounding it, brought a previously secret intelligence-gathering technique to public attention and brought a hitherto unprecedented level of independent scrutiny to the use of this covert technique. It established a tribunal where complaints could be heard and a set of rules that (with just a little modification in relation to CHIS) underpin covert policing today. For example, although distinct activities require different levels of authority, just as in 1985, permission to conduct any one of them is given only when it can be shown that other methods are not feasible or have been tried and failed. As will be demonstrated later, neither the new rules nor the tribunal would go far enough to satisfy critics, but IOCA signalled an important shift in the Home Office's position.

The admissibility of intercept material is a topic regularly revisited because if the product were allowed, it usually would represent the best evidence available.[13] However, any doubt that IOCA was more about preserving the status quo than protecting individual freedoms was removed by the finding in the case of *R vs Preston et al* (HL 5 Nov 1993). *Preston* confirmed IOCA's central purpose as the protection of information about the authorisation of the intercept, the procedure and the intercept product. Under what have come to be known as the Preston Rules, the police cannot be compelled to disclose intercept material either to the prosecution or to the defence; they are obliged only to deliver what became known as a Preston Briefing to the prosecution (CPS, 2015b).[14]

Current legislative regime

Currently, the two most significant pieces of legislation for police intelligence practice are Part III Police Act 1997 and the Regulation of Investigatory Powers Act 2000 (RIPA) (as amended by various orders, discussed later). The focus here is on how they have shaped that practice and the policing institution today.[15]

Part III Police Act 1997

Part III of the Act resolved the anomaly that had existed since 1989, namely that the bugging activities of the SIAs were regulated, but that those same activities carried out by the police were not.[16] It provides statutory authority for covert entry or interference with property by the police in circumstances that otherwise would amount to offences of trespass or criminal damage. That includes, for example, trespassing by covertly searching a home or by damaging a car while fitting a listening device. Arguably, any such activity carried out before the 1997 Act by the police was a de facto breach of Article 8 ECHR, although due to the secrecy surrounding this kind of work few breaches ever came to light. McKay (2011, p.2) has argued that the 1997 Act can be traced back to the anticipated judgement in *Govell vs the UK* (App. No. 27237/95, 14 January 1998). Govell complained that covert police surveillance represented an unjustified interference with his privacy. Unable to seek redress in the UK because the surveillance had been properly conducted under existing Home Office guidelines (Home Office, 1984),[17] Govell took his case to the ECtHR. There, judges held that there had been an unjustified interference with his Article 8 rights. The case later was relied upon in the much more well-known case (at least among police officers), *Khan vs the UK* ([2001] 31 EHRR 1016). Just as in *Malone* and *Govell,* the court ruled that the absence of legal authority or precedent for the police surveillance activity meant there was a clear violation of Article 8.

Surrendering to Europe

Part III was a significant piece of legislation, but the Home Office's obvious short-termism in addressing the specific issues raised by these cases, rather than taking steps to overhaul the wider legislative and procedural framework, was never going to be a sufficient long-term response. Intelligence work and covert policing activities (interception of communications, property interference and trespass aside) continued to be regulated by the 1984 Home Office guidelines, even though there was a significant anxiety both within and without the service that they were not fit for purpose. It was plain that developments in communication technologies (not least the internet and the World Wide Web) were likely to diminish the utility of IOCA. That became even more obvious after another defeat in ECtHR in the case *of Halford vs the UK* (20605/92 [1997] ECHR 32, 25 June 1997). Ironically, the complaint came from a senior British police officer, Alison Halford, who alleged that her employers intercepted her private and office telephone calls, and therefore violated her Article 8 right to privacy, so that they could obtain information to use against her in sex discrimination proceedings.

ECtHR found there had been a violation of Article 8 in relation to calls made on Halford's office telephones. Unsurprisingly, given the court's findings in *Govell* and *Khan*, it also held that there was a violation of Article 13. The case turned on whether Halford had a right to privacy under the Convention in her use of private telecommunication systems, which were not regulated by IOCA. Relying on the test it had applied in *Malone*, the court determined that the answer indisputably was 'yes'. Thus the short-sightedness of the Home Office first in delivering a piece of legislation, IOCA, that fitted the circumstances only of the *Malone* judgement, and second in delivering a piece of legislation, Part III Police Act, tailored to the circumstances of *Govell* and *Khan*, was forcefully brought home to it. It has been argued that it was rapid change in the telecommunications industry that in 1999 prompted a government consultation on the need for new powers (see, for example, Ward and Horne, 2015). *Halford* clearly demonstrates that was a factor but it also made it only too plain that to meet the requirements of HRA, the UK needed more comprehensive legislation and it needed it quickly if it wanted to avoid further embarrassing defeats in ECtHR. Thus RIPA was enacted with as much unseemly haste as IOCA before it.

In July 2014, the legislative framework was further strengthened by the addition of the Data Retention and Investigatory Powers Act (DRIPA). Yet again, the Act was a response to events that should have been foreseen. In this case, the Court of Justice of the European Union's (CJEU) repeal of powers the UK traditionally had relied upon for the retention of communications data. UK legislation was fast-tracked to ensure that the police and SIAs maintained access to individuals' phone and internet records. The government was heavily criticised for bypassing normal protocols by civil liberties groups and by members of parliament (MPs) from all parties. For a while, emotions ran high; MPs David Davis and Tom Watson (backed by campaign group Liberty) launched a legal challenge on the basis that DRIPA did not respect citizens' rights. However, without the Act the government would have been forced either to destroy the records its agencies held or risk further embarrassment in ECtHR.

Regulation of Investigatory Powers Act 2000

RIPA provides an elaborate set of statutory arrangements for covert investigative practice. In some circumstances, limited powers are extended to other public authorities, though their use must be approved in advance by a magistrate (Protection of Freedoms Act 2012).

Fundamentally, RIPA mirrored IOCA; a violation may be justified if it is proportionate, in accordance with law, and:

- either necessary to protect
  - national security
  - public safety or
  - the economic wellbeing of the country; or
- to prevent
  - disorder or crime, or
- to protect
  - health or morals
  - rights and freedoms of others.

There may be sympathy for the views of one commentator that in this context 'successive pieces of legislation appear to simply rubber stamp or extend existing practice' (Taylor, 2002, p.73), and to the view of a second that RIPA 'represents the continued adherence to the tradition of minimal compliance with overriding external principles which is so favoured by legislators in Westminster' (Bhatt, 2006, p.285).

Drafting RIPA was not the onerous task one might imagine because the Act largely represents a regurgitation of IOCA, the 1984 guidelines and the ACPO/HMCE/NCIS/NCS Manual of Standards for Covert Investigation (first published in 1999), and, although there are some changes to practice, these represent tinkering at the margins much more than substantial reforms. For example, in the context of the interception of communications, there is the same expectation that intercept material will be destroyed. Conversely, RIPA allows that in 'exceptional circumstances', senior prosecutors and judges may to be given access to material that has not yet been destroyed to determine (in the former case) that the prosecution is fair or (in the latter) in the interests of a fair trial. It remains true that material will never be used in evidence and should never be disclosed to the defence, but, as *Malone* demonstrated, human frailty is found everywhere.

RIPA could be celebrated as the product of close collaboration between the Home Office and the agencies that, in the first instance, were expected to implement the Act. Some may believe that was a sensible way to approach the challenge of drafting the legislation, but it did little to dispel the view (expressed, for example, by Taylor, 2002 and Spencer, 2009) that RIPA and its codes represented a defence of state power more than a meaningful commitment to human rights and liberties. It did provide another example of the ways in which the policing institution has been a significant actor in structuring and shaping political behaviour and (in this case) law.

The positives for the police in this context are obvious: the new Act effectively meant 'business as usual', although it demanded a much more comprehensive record-keeping system and that very much added to the bureaucratic, process-driven nature of the work. Critics have argued that the Act allows for too much latitude in the authorisation of surveillance activity (see Hirsch, 2002, p.1328). Certainly, there is wooliness around some of its provisions. For example, RIPA is permissive legislation: evidence gained other than in accordance with the Act still may be allowed in judicial proceedings. RIPA does not make the activity unlawful, but such evidence runs the risk of being ruled as inadmissible (under Section 78 PACE Police and Criminal Evidence Act 1984). That was confirmed in 2006 by the Investigatory Powers Tribunal (IPT) which ruled that, 'there is no general prohibition in RIPA against conducting directed surveillance without RIPA authorisation' (IPT, cited in Ward and Horne, 2015, pp.6-7). Other questions of individual competence or ethics may arise if RIPA rules are not followed, but irregular activity will never be unlawful per se.

RIPA codes of practice

These codes underpin covert investigation. Initially, justly criticised as reiterations of the legislation, they have been updated to include regulatory and procedural reforms (see Home Office, 2014a). For example, the 2014 version of the codes include amendments to RIPA made by the Regulation of Investigatory Powers (Extension of Authorisation Provisions: Legal Consultations) Order 2010, the Protection of Freedoms Act 2012 and the Regulation of Investigatory Powers (Covert Human Intelligence Sources: Relevant Sources) Order 2013. Moreover, a period of public consultation on a new code for equipment interference (under Part III RIPA) recently ended. It is expected that the code will set new standards for the use of techniques such as computer hacking.

The codes can have far-reaching implications for practice. For example, the 2010 Order instructs the police to consider surveillance as 'intrusive' rather than 'directed' (and therefore subject to additional safeguards) if it seeks to monitor a legal consultation. The 2012 Act requires public authorities other than law enforcement agencies to seek judicial approval before attempting to access communications data or carrying out surveillance. In the wake of the Mark Kennedy and Bob Lambert affairs, the 2013 Order rebrands an undercover officer as a 'relevant source' and directs that long-term deployments must be approved by a surveillance commissioner or (in cases where information that may be subject to legal privilege is sought) the relevant Secretary of State.

Watching the watchers

The oversight regime is composed of seven separate bodies, which are expected to monitor the lawful exercise of investigative powers by public authorities. They are:

• Interception of Communications Commissioner (IOCC);
• Chief Surveillance Commissioner (CSC);
• Intelligence Services Commissioner;
• Information Commissioner;
• Surveillance Camera Commissioner;
• Commissioner for the Retention and Use of Biometric Material;
• Investigatory Powers Tribunal (IPT).[18]

This analysis focuses on those that have the greatest significance in this context: the interception and surveillance commissioners (the IOCC and CSC respectively).

Interception of Communications Commissioner

At six-monthly intervals, the IOCC carries out audits of the interception of the content of communications and also the acquisition and disclosure of communications data under Part I RIPA by any agency. The IOCC cannot provide a full picture of relevant activity for operational security reasons and (in relation to interception) by the RIPA provisions themselves. Nonetheless, with careful reading, the reports do provide some understanding of the milieu. For example, the IOCC's 2015 report reveals that some Part I applications did not meet the key necessity and/or proportionality tests. Post-Snowden, it is easy to see why the commissioner would note that that there was 'More the intelligence agencies, police forces and law enforcement could do, and should do, to better inform the public about how they use their powers under RIPA 2000, why they need these intrusive powers and, why additional powers might be required' (IOCC, 2015, p.10). Given the explicit responsibility of the IOCC to oversee and keep under review the interception of communications and the acquisition of communications data by SIAs, police forces and other public authorities, one equally might question whether there was more that the IOCC could have done to challenge the police and (particularly) the SIAs before Snowden brought their activities to public attention.

Chief Surveillance Commissioner

The CSC heads the Office of Surveillance Commissioners, which annually reviews public authorities' use of powers under Part III of the Police Act 1997 and Parts II and III of RIPA in England, Wales and Scotland. In some cases, the prior authority of a surveillance commissioner must be sought before activity can be undertaken, but all activity (requiring prior authority or not) must be reported (see McKay, 2011).[19] The CSC's reports are rich sources of data. For example, the 2014 report notes a significant fall in the number of directed surveillance authorisations granted to law enforcement agencies over the past 10 years (CSC, 2015, p.11). Similarly, CHIS recruitment has shown that same downward trend over the same period (CSC, 2015, p.13).

What these trends mean for practice is a matter of conjecture. They might bring comfort to critics of the legislation or might even imply the police have found new ways to collect the information they need (through, for example, open source or social media research). Rather than providing one answer, this study suggests those falls can be attributed to a number of factors, including: a greater focus on quality than quantity (particularly in the investigation of serious and organised crime); budgetary constraints on CHIS management units; an increasing aversion to the risks that this kind of work brings; a steadily shrinking pool of staff with the requisite skills, knowledge, and abilities to manage CHIS properly; and (more broadly) police budgets reduced across the board by at least 20%.

In that same report, the CSC commented *inter alia* on the shortcomings of some applicants and authorising officers. Some of the reports seen by the CSC's inspectors included 'unsubstantiated and brief, or, conversely, excessively detailed intelligence cases … poor proportionality arguments … the obvious "cut and paste" content of reviews of long-running operations … and the overly formulaic assessment of the potential for collateral intrusion' (CSC, 2015, p.22). Highlighting the importance of this last point, a statutory requirement, the commissioner noted that there were 'before the courts matters which appear to have involved collateral intrusion of the most intimate nature'. (CSC, 2015, p.22). That suggests that ECHR rights remain under threat and that a more robust system of pre-authorisation scrutiny is needed.

RIPA's long goodbye

Both RIPA and the oversight regime itself recently have come in for heavy criticism and it is difficult to see either surviving in their current form. The ISC's inquiry into the Snowden leak was broadened into an investigation into the full range of SIAs' intrusive capabilities, in terms not only of scale and *modus operandi*, but also the extent to which the existing legislation adequately defined and constrained those capabilities (ISC, 2015). In March 2015, the ISC reported that the legal framework had developed 'piecemeal' and it had 'serious concerns about the resulting lack of transparency, which is not in the public interest'. It called for 'a new, transparent legal framework' (ISC, 2015, p.2).

As part of the coalition government's deal with the other major political parties over the passage of DRIPA, the independent reviewer of terrorism legislation, David Anderson QC, was commissioned to review investigatory powers. Published in June 2015, his report shifted the focus from the police and SIAs and on to the legislation and those who oversee those powers. Substantially reflecting the view expressed in this analysis, Anderson opined that:

> RIPA, obscure since its inception, has been patched up so many times as to make it incomprehensible to all but a tiny band of initiates. A multitude of alternative powers, some of them without statutory safeguards, confuse the picture further. This state of affairs is undemocratic, unnecessary and – in the long run – intolerable. (Anderson, 2015, p.8)

Anderson was supported in that view by many of the submissions he received from practitioners, jurists and lobbyists, which 'demonstrated limited trust in the oversight mechanisms' (Anderson, 2015, pp.235-6). The commissioner system, across the board, also was criticised as fractured, insular, remote and ineffective, its appointments subject to the whim of the Executive and its scrutiny of RIPA-related activity 'inadequate' (Anderson, 2015, p.238). Moreover, the IPT was condemned as bureaucratic, limited and lacking transparency. Anderson recommended *inter alia* that all surveillance activity should be subject to judicial approval as it is in other European states, that there should be a unified oversight system, and that the powers of the IPT should be strengthened substantially (Anderson, 2015).

Within weeks of Anderson's report, a second independent surveillance review was published (RUSI, 2015).[20] This review was conducted by a 12-strong panel that included former heads of MI5, MI6, and GCHQ and distinguished academics. Its terms of reference were, in the light of the Snowden revelations, to consider the legality of UK surveillance programmes and the effectiveness of the oversight regime, and to suggest reforms. Primarily, the panel was concerned with 'the interception and use of private communications and related data' by the police and SIAs. Like Anderson's review, the RUSI report is detailed, comprehensive and lengthy, and contains a wealth of interesting data. The panel rejected most of Snowden's allegations, but, just like Anderson, it agreed that 'the present legal framework authorising the interception of communications is unclear, has not kept pace with developments in communications technology, and does not serve either the government or members of the public satisfactorily. A new, comprehensive and clearer legal framework is required' (RUSI, 2015, pp.xi-xii).

The initial response of government to the Anderson review was lukewarm; there were no promises to accept his findings, and, furthermore there was an obvious reluctance to accede to one of his main recommendations to transfer power from politicians to judges. The government response to the RUSI report has been more muted and it remains unclear just how committed it is to meaningful change. A Bill to replace RIPA will be introduced sometime in the next parliamentary session. For all the reasons explored in this chapter, it is to be hoped that the new legislation will be considered much more carefully than that which has gone before it.

Summary

The current legislative framework is the product of a series of step-changes linked to political and/or judicial matters over the past 20 years, essentially a sequence of defensive acts that ceded ground only incrementally to advocates of greater transparency and accountability. Central to those developments was ECtHR. The evidence suggests that there never has been much enthusiasm within the executive for change; successive governments have found themselves at odds with ECtHR over the lawfulness of the work. There is disappointment in some quarters that the UK still has not fully embraced ECHR and does not subscribe to judicial oversight of all planned intelligence activity. Hitherto, the dominant political view seems to have been that the UK is human rights-compliant *enough*. The current oversight system provides an element of scrutiny of investigatory powers. However, there is a growing and increasingly influential body of opinion that believes that substantial change to both the legislative and oversight frameworks is essential. Given the posture adopted by the government, it can safely be forecast that change is on the way, even if the detail of that change can only be guessed at.

Notes

[1] Detailed practice-focused analyses already have been published by, for example, Harfield and Harfield (2008, 2012) and an authoritative analysis of covert policing law and its practice in England and Wales has been produced by McKay (2011, 2015 [2nd edn]). Those texts are widely available. Ward and Horne's (2015) parliamentary briefing note provides an excellent summary of the legal issues surrounding surveillance and interception. It is available online at http://researchbriefings.parliament.uk/ResearchBriefing/Summary/SN06332#fullreport

[2] Case law bearing on intelligence work goes back to 1794 (the ruling in the case of *R vs Hardy*, to protect the identity of an informer), but as only a fraction of intelligence work results in prosecution the work is rarely addressed in judicial proceedings.

[3] Brodeur's distinction between high and low policing functions (1983) is acknowledged. The terms distinguish between the degrees of politics attached to different policing activities: neither high nor low in that context are absolutes.

[4] Others included developments in communication and other technologies, post-Scarman communitarianism within police management and sustained challenge from jurists on the grounds of fairness.

[5] Some have argued that the Common Informers Act 1951 was the first.

[6] In relation to legal proceedings, access to sensitive personal data also may be obtained.

[7] See the companion website for further discussion of DPA principles.

[8] The UK played a key role in drafting the Convention. Citizens have had right of petition since 1966.

[9] The IPT maintains a full list of authorities and the extent of their powers under RIPA.

[10] As in the case of Aso Mohammed Ibrahim, an Iraqi asylum-seeker convicted in 2003 of killing a child in a road traffic accident. At the time, Ibrahim had no licence, drove recklessly and also fled the scene.

[11] See also the judgement in *Van Colle vs the UK*, which emphasises the high threshold for this test.

[12] Although ECHR was not incorporated into UK law until the enactment of the Human Rights Act 1998, the UK still could be held in violation as it was a signatory to the original 1950 agreement.

13 Intercept material can be used in evidence if it is collected under prison rules or collected abroad and both parties are abroad (*R vs Aujla* [1998] 2 Cr App R 16).

14 The briefing confirms that interception was carried out, that the warrant was lawfully issued by the Home Secretary, that the intercept product has been destroyed and that nobody any longer has an accurate recollection of the intercepted material. Those arrangements largely were unchanged by RIPA.

15 This book cannot capture all the nuances and intricacies of the legislation. See McKay (2011, 2015) for detailed legal analyses.

16 Following the enactment of the Intelligence Services Act 1989.

17 Chief or assistant chief constables were entitled to authorise the use of such devices provided that: the investigation concerned serious crime; normal methods of investigation had been tried and failed, or were unlikely to succeed if tried; there was good reason to think its use would lead to an arrest and conviction, or to the prevention of terrorism; and the use of equipment had to be operationally feasible. The authorising officer also had to be satisfied that the degree of intrusion was commensurate with the seriousness of the offence under investigation.

18 The post of Investigatory Powers Commissioner for Northern Ireland also was created, but the post has never been filled.

19 This includes where authorisation for intrusive surveillance is sought and where legally privileged information may be found.

20 The review was commissioned by Nick Clegg in his role as Deputy Prime Minister of the coalition government.

Further reading

Anderson, D (2015), *A Question of Trust — Report of the Investigatory Powers Review*. London: Anderson.

McKay, S (2015), *Covert Policing Law and Practice* (2nd Edn.). London: OUP.

RUSI (2015), *Democratic Licence to Operate, Report of the Independent Surveillance Review*. London: RUSI.

FIVE

Organisational intelligence processes

Introduction

The police collect huge quantities of data in many different forms. Determining what is of value and what is not is an undertaking that requires significant resources as well as significant expertise. For data judged as valuable, the initial concerns are for its provenance and for the safety of its source. The police use a standard model to validate and sort the information and also to carry out a 'first-cut' risk assessment. Once the information is entered into the police system, other factors, such as the protection of the data while it is being transmitted or stored, come to the fore. Those processes are examined here.

National Intelligence Model (NIM)

Conceptually consistent, police intelligence work is underpinned by the intelligence cycle, the same model used for many years by law enforcement agencies and SIAs worldwide.[1] At the beginning of this century, UK policing built what was intended to be a more effective a management structure, the NIM, on to that foundation. Essentially, an elaboration of the standard cycle, NIM was an attempt to fuse intelligence work with business processes. Ultimately, the aim was to achieve more with less, something that arguably is even more necessary today. Despite the rhetoric, significant failings in NIM and its implementation undermined meaningful acceptance of it beyond the intelligence milieu. NIM did not fundamentally change the police service as its architects intended, nor did it provide the business-oriented proactive focus that was expected; intelligence work continued to be afforded low status and the reactive policing paradigm continued to dominate.

Broadly, police intelligence staff welcomed NIM for the structure it brought to their work, but the model had little meaningful impact beyond that milieu. Even when it was being pushed hard by a section of the service elite, many practitioners felt that the operational world needed something simpler – something less likely to threaten traditional structures and practices and more easily understood by frontline cops (see James, 2013). When the impetus for change faded, so too did NIM, from organisational consciousness even if the rhetoric and NIM-derived labels attached to some intelligence processes suggested otherwise. Those labels and the enthusiasm for the model in the intelligence world meant that even though few saw it as viable, NIM remained visible. Moreover (thanks to the lobbying of the service elite during the implementation process), its statutory codification meant that NIM always was referenced in policing policy.

Between 2000 and 2011, NIM was the subject of a number of reviews and thematic inspections; none resulted in any significant changes to the model. The NIM narrative might have ended there, but there were just enough believers in the intelligence world, with enough influence in the wider organisation, that in 2013 they were able to persuade the organisation to commission a review of NIM. That review and its findings are analysed in this chapter.

NIM in purdah

Rather than using NIM to deliver better outcomes, many forces implemented just enough of the model to provide a veneer of compliance that insulated them from sanction, and no more. Fundamentally, there never was the support for NIM that the rhetoric suggested; many saw its merits, but few, if any, were prepared to make the significant structural changes to their forces that full compliance with the model demanded. Police commanders did not intend to mislead. Equally, time and events have shown that there was no political will to call them out for their prevarication. The Home Office and police authorities largely were passive, content to trust the professional judgement of the police (not a position that either the former or the latter – now replaced by Police and Crime Commissioners – would be likely to adopt today).

For all the energy expended on NIM by some of the service elite, it is wholly understandable that individual commanders would choose the status quo; their forces traditionally had operated the intelligence cycle and motivated by the dominant ethos in the public sector, New Public Management, they already had processes in place to help them apportion their resources and direct action. As Figure 5.1 shows, where adopted, NIM processes (the outer ring of the figure) conceivably might have added a more business-oriented factor to the equation, but fundamentally they would not have added very much to the basic intelligence or planning processes. Commanders' failure to embrace a model that ACPO, their own representative body, had developed for the service may have been perceived by some as less than collegial, but it was not financially or reputationally injurious to them or their forces. The greatest costs were incurred by those who chose to comply, in terms both of actual expenditure and also opportunity costs, as more layers of bureaucracy were added to systems already creaking under the weight of it.

Figure 5.1: Comparing intelligence cycle and NIM processes

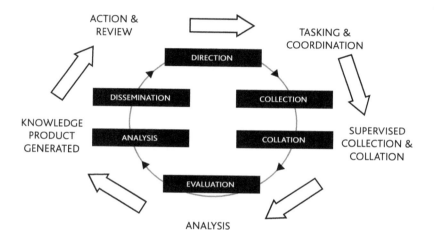

For a while, NIM's future seemed bleak. Arguably, without its statutory codification, and like so many other transformational policing initiatives long faded from individual and organisational consciousness, it would have ebbed away leaving just a few traces here and there to act, for the less than fully employed, as triggers for coffee-shop banter or, for the next generation of policy entrepreneurs, as stimuli for ground-breaking policing initiatives. However, as reported in the aftermath of the Soham murders (Bichard, 2004),[2] there remained a clear and obvious need for significant improvements in police information and intelligence management systems, which NIM 'compliance' had not addressed. That remains true today; in a recent report on an inspection of police information management, 'a real and pressing need for greater attention to be paid to the management of police information' was revealed (HMIC, 2015, p.14).

In the first study of NIM (2003-7), a senior police officer said that despite the continuing problems in information management and his force's rejection of the model, the unstinting efforts of a small number of 'inspirational individuals' committed to the professionalisation of intelligence work, gave him hope that it could yet have a positive impact. Subsequent events suggest that there were enough of those individuals in forces and at NPIA to keep NIM on decision makers' agendas and eventually to convince enough of them of the need for change. The case for the NIM (or at least a modified form of it) seemed to gain traction following an overhaul of the model in 2011 by NPIA (NPIA, 2011). Even though this restatement of NIM represented a significant downgrading of the grand plan, it seemed to breathe new life into it. A key factor was that in its revised form, the NIM was process-focused and full compliance no longer required prospective adopters to commit to significant (and no doubt expensive) structural change.

NIM review 2012

Throughout 2012, a service-wide consultation on the future of the model revealed support for its principles but doubts about its continuing utility without meaningful change. Common complaints were the inflexibility of its structure, its limited capacity for wider inclusion (particularly outside of policing) and the challenges of integrating NIM with other models of policing (such as COMPSTAT [a management philosophy committed to data analysis, targeted interventions, and commanders personal responsibility for crime reduction] and the neighbourhood policing programme). The efforts of the inspired few eventually gathered enough support to merit the establishment of an ACPO team to work with NPIA to review the NIM and, in October 2012, that led to a NIM review conference (more accurately a workshop) at the NPIA conference centre in Leicestershire.

The conference was attended by more than 150 invited delegates. That included senior intelligence leads from 40 police forces, and delegates from various national law enforcement agencies, higher education institutions, 29 government agencies and many other public authorities. It was chaired by a chief constable, the ACPO intelligence lead, and an assistant chief constable, the ACPO NIM lead, which provided just the kind of executive endorsement that is essential in hierarchical bureaucracies. SOCA had rejected NIM as an organising framework for its operations, so it was significant too that one of the delegates was the newly appointed Director-General of the NCA, who, in his keynote speech, backed the review and indicated that the NCA would integrate a revised model into its work.

Delegates responded to questions about NIM's strengths and weaknesses and about their views on a new version of the model. Additionally, they gave their views on the barriers to effective information sharing, a national intelligence strategy and the management of covert policing more generally. Altogether, those running the conference collected more than 2,000 individual responses that were used to inform the development of a roadmap for reforming NIM. Most delegates wanted NIM to be simplified and streamlined. Other concerns were the lack of training and other opportunities for personal and career development, the doubts over intelligence as a profession, the need for greater buy-in from senior leaders and the need for greater interoperability with partners. Many responses confirmed the continued existence of the intelligence pathologies described in Chapter One.

Some delegates also expressed concern over the prospect of further cuts in police budgets and the identification by some forces of intelligence work as a back-office function. That is a thorny issue because equally good cases probably can be made by both sides; in an era when police forces are under such considerable pressure to cut costs, it is no surprise to see some identify their intelligence units as sites where savings can be made. Given the inadequacies identified over many years by scholars and the service alike, there may be good grounds for believing that to be true. Before moving on to explain some of the results of all that intellectual endeavour, it is worth reflecting on the review process.

The police organisation is conservative to its core and while this kind of consultation is not unique, it is unusual to see police decision makers being quite so democratic and participative. Those familiar with the NIM narrative will know that the service took the diametrically opposite approach when it introduced the model. Then its architects, with the best of intentions, deliberately selected a top-down approach aimed at senior leaders and managers, which did not engage with the staff expected to operate the model in any meaningful way. Attempts to market the NIM in forces extended only to the short-term provision of hands-on support in relatively few sites and the production (by the ACPO NIM implementation team) of a NIM CD-ROM, thought by those who viewed it as impenetrable as the NIM manual that had preceded it.

This was by no means the only problem with NIM, but without that buy-in from the ground floor there was never any measure of popular demand for it. The workforce largely was apathetic; implementation was all push and no pull and it became a toss-up over which side would win out. Although few saw the struggle in those terms, there never really was much heat in the debate. No attempts were made to sabotage the grand plan; it simply was widely ignored. Eventually, it became a question of 'when' not 'if' the organisational energy behind NIM would be exhausted and the service would move on to the next challenge. With national security dominating the policing agenda in the new millennium, the answer was 'Not very long'.

It is against that background that the efforts of those officers and staff in forces, in other law enforcement agencies and in the CoP who have managed to breathe new life into the NIM and consequently into police intelligence work more widely should be judged. Their efforts have been considerable; the persistence and acumen they have demonstrated in bringing together UK intelligence practitioners, academics and intelligence professionals from elsewhere in the world have established a solid foundation for the programmes they now pursue. One of their key aims was that initial gains should be sustained. They have therefore put significant effort into consensus building, developing relationships with individuals and institutions outside of the policing bubble. Those endeavours have already begun to bear fruit, with the launch of new postgraduate qualifications in intelligence in two UK universities and police staff exchanges with intelligence training providers in the US. The evidence collected in the course of the review also has given support to those seeking to professionalise intelligence work through the IPP and ancillary initiatives.

NIM today

The current iteration of NIM is very different. Originally, compliance required the achievement of 135 minimum standards. The new version sets out just four, as follows:

- the organisation should have governance and command structures;
- it should demonstrate knowledge management;
- it should gather information and make use of intelligence;
- it should have tasking and coordinating (T&C) processes.

Some may feel that these standards are now so broad as to be almost meaningless, but they are underpinned by a framework of definitions and advice that may guide organisations' plans for the model. For example, the broadest and most anodyne of the four standards – that the organisation should demonstrate knowledge management – requires organisations to provide staff with access to relevant legislation and guidance and to have processes in place for reviewing and updating staff knowledge. There also are a host of definitions and further advisories, but none of these is mandatory. This is a very different, almost *laissez faire*, approach.

Leadership in public institutions has been the subject of inquiry for many years. The particular significance of this episode is the contrast between this approach and the autocratic leadership model that characterised NIM's first iteration and the rational-legal model that dominates the policing world. A leadership style is *laissez faire* if its supporters 'have total freedom to select and to set their own objectives and to monitor their own work' (Kurfi, cited in Feldman, 2012, p.4). This analysis demonstrates the participative style of the review, but it would be too much of a stretch to suggest that democracy extends quite that far in policing. This kind of process is unlikely to become the norm, but, given the criticism the service has received over NIM (see, for example, Kleiven, 2005), its willingness to consult widely, to communicate directly with practitioners and the wider intelligence community, and to respond to feedback in a profound way merits recognition.

The intelligence milieu today is rather different from that which existed in the 1990s when the NIM was in embryonic form. Perhaps the most significant changes to that environment have been brought about by HRA and RIPA.[3] Between them, the Acts created a 'common legal environment' (DiMaggio and Powell, 1983, p.150), which significantly affected the police organisation and many aspects of intelligence work. HRA imposes a duty on the police to put human rights principles at the heart of all of their operations. RIPA demands compliance with a suite of statutory arrangements that determine the conduct of covert investigations. Certainly, the Acts impose an oversight regime that just did not exist at the beginning of the century.

Developing intelligence

Confidentiality, provenance and sanitisation are key terms in intelligence development. Each of those terms is critically analysed here.

Confidentiality of sources

The police have a common law duty to maintain the confidentiality of their information sources. Routinely, the police apply the long-established 'neither confirm nor deny' principle in relation to their use of covert methodology, sensitive information or sources. Like all UK public authorities, they also must comply with relevant statutory controls designed either (depending on the particular circumstances) to restrict or facilitate access to data such as DPA and FOIA. The Criminal Procedure and Investigations Act 1996 (CIPA), and associated codes, is particularly important because it stipulates that any material relevant to criminal proceedings is recorded, retained and revealed to the Crown Prosecution Service (CPS).[4] The CPS has a statutory duty to disclose to the defendant's legal representatives any material that may assist the defence or undermine the prosecution. Relevant material includes obvious items, such as surveillance and CHIS logs, communications data requests, RIPA applications and authorisations. It also could include less obvious material, such as a recording of a call to a police control room, a sketch map of a crime scene drawn by an officer as an *aide mémoire* or details of a credit check carried out on a suspect. Material must be revealed to the defence if it 'tends to show a fact inconsistent with the elements of the case that must be proved by the prosecution' (CPS, 2015a, p.1). For example, disclosure would be made if a description of a defendant recorded in a surveillance log manifestly did not fit the person in the dock in the subsequent court proceedings.

Informers have historically received the protection of the law. Neither the identity of an informer nor anything that may lead to their identification may be disclosed by witnesses in criminal proceedings. The justification extends beyond the safety of the individual informer. In *R vs Hennessy* [1978] 68 Cr. App. R419, Lord Justice Lawson ruled that 'The courts appreciate the need to protect the identity of informers not only for their own safety but to ensure that the supply of information about criminal activities does not dry up.' There is an exception to the general rule; it may be overturned if the disclosure either of the identity of the informer or the information they provide is the critical factor in determining the innocence of the accused – see *Marks vs Beyfus* (1890) 25 QBD 494.

In consequence of *R vs Rankine* [1986] QB 861 and *R vs Johnson* [1988] 1 WLR 1377, the identity of observation points and any individuals who permit their premises to be used as such are similarly protected.[5] Ordinarily, such matters – indeed any relating to the disclosure of intelligence material – are dealt with according to the legal principle of public interest. In cases where this may be at issue, a formal public interest immunity (PII) hearing usually takes place before trial (or during a trial in the absence of the jury if a PII issue is identified in the course of the proceedings). Applying this principle enables courts to reconcile conflicting public interests: the right of a defendant to fair trial and the right of the state to use covert methods to prevent or detect crime.[6]

Evaluating information

Every piece of information merits evaluation because one cannot know the future and the risk of overlooking an important piece of the jigsaw always is present. While in some situations it may immediately be apparent that some form of investigation or legal process will follow (and adherence to CPIA must be made a priority), in others the outcome is much less certain and information may not be recognised as relevant until long after the initial event. The process of evaluation is in itself difficult and time-consuming. With so many possible variables, ultimately what is appropriate depends on a subjective test, the outcome of which is dependent *inter alia* on context, the professional and life skills of the receiver and other existential (and perhaps technological) factors as much as it is on logic or rationality. Given the quantity and variety of data collected, it would be impossible to formulate a rule for each and every situation that may arise. Therefore, it may be wholly understandable that APP guidance on this important point should be as anodyne and equivocal as 'the evaluation should be appropriate to the policing purpose for which [the information] was collected and recorded' (CoP, 2013a, p.1). Further guidance stresses the importance of proportionality; for example, 'A crime-in-action normally requires a faster response than an abandoned vehicle report' (CoP, 2013b, p.1). However, it is a concern that the service considers that professional police officers need such advice.

It is contended throughout this book that policing is anti-intellectual; this a good example of the kind of overly simplistic instrumentalism that pervades policing. The guidance fulfils the organisation's purpose – essentially, staff have been told what to do so there is neither a policy nor a management vacuum – but it is rather less useful for those who may later be called on to justify their decisions. Largely, that is because the independent variable, the relevant policing purpose, often cannot be known. In the context of intelligence work, even if a single purpose is known, the information also may have value for many other purposes. Policing reflects life; both are full of unknowns. It may be weeks, months or even years before it is known whether a particular piece of information has intrinsic value, instrumental value, both intrinsic and instrumental value, or no value at all.

Provenance

Provenance is derived from the French word *provenir*, which means to proceed from or to come from. Used in the classic sense, it describes a timeline of the ownership, custodianship or setting of a work of art, but the term has come to be used in a wide range of fields including the natural sciences, archival research and in database theory (where the complementary terms 'pedigree' and 'lineage' also are used – see Buneman et al, 2001). Ultimately, provenance is the process by which one seeks context for, and corroboration of, the authenticity of the object of inquiry by tracing its history, paying particular attention to the absence or existence of evidence of ownership, sale or purchase, and to storage or archival records.

Establishing the provenance of a piece of information represents a first-cut risk analysis; it is an essential step both in judging its utility and the risks involved in going on to use it. Provenance is analogous to the terms 'chain of custody' and 'chain of evidence' used in criminal investigations and legal proceedings. In both cases, the integrity of the material collected is established and maintained by ensuring that detailed records are kept, that its antecedents are investigated fully, and, while in the hands of (in this case) the police, that any changes in its condition are recorded. The process can be complicated, but in the intelligence context provenance usually can be determined by obtaining answers to four very simple questions, namely:

- How does the source know the information?
- Who else knows it?
- When did they first know the information to be correct?
- When did they last know it to be correct?

People naturally attribute greater value to information based on knowledge than on belief. Therefore, if the person providing the information (the CHIS) saw contraband with their own eyes, their information usually would be considered more reliable than if they had received the same information second-hand. There is a persuasive philosophical argument that knowledge need not be better than belief if an individual is indifferent to its veracity (see, for example, Pillar, 2009).[7] As CHIS usually is motivated by the prospect of reward, that epistemological trap usually can safely be avoided (even if the ethical and legal minefields that lie in wait cannot be negotiated so easily), but there remain supplementary questions to be answered about the nature of the CHIS's knowledge. These include 'What is their involvement in the crime?', 'What is their motivation for providing the information?' and 'Can their information be corroborated in any way?'

The answer to the question 'Who else knows the information?' is critical in determining the level of risk to the informer. Plans for action must fulfil the police's duty of care. If the information is known only to the CHIS, that might be considered a compelling reason not to act without corroboration or the use of subterfuge because the associated risk could not otherwise easily be mitigated. Conversely, if the CHIS knows that the offender has been touting goods around local pubs and clubs, many people could know of their existence and that would dramatically reduce the risks associated with action. The timeframe is extremely important. If the CHIS has delayed passing the information on, it may already be out of date. That also raises questions about the CHIS's part in the crime and their relationship with the offender. At the other end of the scale, if the information is just minutes old, that might provide some confidence that the offender still is in possession of the contraband, but the CHIS's welfare post-seizure would need to be factored into the operational risk assessment. If their welfare cannot be guaranteed, that again will provide cause for further reflection before action.

If a CHIS is harmed as a result of something the police do (or should have done and did not), they would not automatically be able to seek redress through the courts. It largely is accepted that civil proceedings against chief officers for a negligent investigation by their forces usually will fail. However, in *Swinney vs Chief Constable of Northumbria* [1996] 3 All ER 449, LJ Hirst held that was not a blanket immunity. Where negligence was exceptional in character, other public policy issues, such as 'the need to … protect informers, and to encourage them to come forward without an undue fear of the risk that their identity will subsequently become known to the suspect or to his associates' had to be considered.

Organised crime group mapping (OCGM)

It has been estimated that there are about 5,500 active organised crime groups operating against the UK, comprising about 37,000 people. Their criminal activity is concentrated in, but not limited to, the country's major commercial hubs: London and the South East; Manchester, Liverpool and the North West; and Birmingham and the West Midlands (Home Office, 2013). OCGM is not a new phenomenon; one of the first models was developed by the Royal Canadian Mounted Police in 2000. The Sleipnir model used a rank-ordered set of attributes to measure the organised crime threat (Strang, 2000). The 19 attributes include corruption, violence, infiltration, expertise and sophistication, which are applied to the known groups, scored, and then those scores extrapolated to produce a ranking. The rationale for that process is that scarce operational resources can be used against the highest ranked (and therefore most dangerous) groups. Sleipnir has spawned many imitations, each claiming to be more accurate and reliable than the last. All seem to suffer from the same flaws: that it is impossible to remove subjectivity from the process and that accurate assessments of the groups' capabilities often rely on technical knowledge (for example, of cybercrime or money laundering) that assessors lack. Although the processes may be flawed, there is no doubting the need for them. The police will never have sufficient resources to combat every organised crime group. Therefore some filtering process will always be necessary. The challenge is to refine the process so that resources are directed to where they are most needed.

Sharing intelligence

There are strict rules for sharing information or intelligence in this environment. Some of those rules, however, are not as clear as they should be nor are they as well understood by practitioners as they might be, and whether they are always followed as scrupulously as they should be is questionable. Raw data should be edited to ensure that its source cannot be identified in a process known as sanitisation. A standard model, the 3x5x2 system, is used by the police to manage that data (CoP, 2013a). Additionally, security classification policies determine how the data should be stored and transmitted.

Sanitisation

'Sanitisation occurs when material is removed from the original information, which explicitly or implicitly identifies a source' (CoP, 2013b, p.1). A confidential source register (CSR) is used (now more accurately a spreadsheet or database) to mask the identity of the source. Sanitisation is a critically important element in source protection. Largely, it involves editing or redacting information or intelligence reports to remove anything that might reveal the source's identity (human or otherwise), thereby reducing the risk of reprisals against the source and also protecting methodologies and tradecraft. Sanitisation does not remove the requirement to record information accurately; the audit trail must be maintained. Often, a CHIS will provide a number of different pieces of information. Each should be recorded under a different CSR reference so as to further limit the chances of identification.

Grading intelligence

All modern intelligence grading systems are based on the 6x6 Admiralty system used extensively in the last century (McDowell, 2009). Traditionally, UK policing used a 5x5x5 system, but in September it was revised and now is more accurately (though it remains to be seen if the phrase will be taken into common usage) a 3x5x2 system. It represents a standard process of assessing police information. The system is not used for all information received by the police. Often, it is entered directly into an intelligence database or some other recording system (for example, as a custody record or crime report). It is used when information is supplied in confidence by a member of the public, by another law enforcement agency or by a CHIS, or is obtained by other covert means (CoP, 2015d). Broadly, the system consists of three elements – the source, the information and the handling code – each of which are assessed to determine the value of the information and the extent to which it may be shared around the organisation or beyond.[8]

Figure 5.2 illustrates how the sanitisation and grading processes typically are applied to an information report.

In light of the foregoing analysis, it may be obvious that the CHIS's name and address should be redacted. However, it may be that Freddie is a nickname known only to Mr Armstrong or to a small number of associates and that also should be removed. The fact that the CHIS is familiar with local bars might suggest that the information has been passed on by a neighbour. The inclusion of the CSR number (randomly

Figure 5.2: Intelligence assessment (the 5x5x5 model)

Original information	Sanitised version	Grading
Jack Armstrong of 29 The Grove reports that a lorry has been parked outside 32 The Grove for the last 15 minutes. The occupant, Freddie, has taken at least 10, boxed, flat-screen televisions into that address. Freddie has lived there for about six months. Mr Armstrong knows that Freddie has been offering to sell electrical goods cheaply in the local bar. Freddie has intimated that the TVs are stolen.	Intelligence suggests that the occupant of 32 The Grove may be in possession of stolen electrical equipment – CSR 237/15/0946	1/A/A3 (indicating that it has been assessed as reliable information that is known to the source and that the sanitised information is cleared for overt use)

generated) identifies where the unredacted report may be found and ensures that the audit trail is maintained.

The 3x5x2 system was introduced to overcome significant shortcomings in the previous system, which tended to encourage conservatism and risk aversion. Under that system, codes were used disproportionately.[9] Research showed that officers and staff who obtained information by covert means or received it in confidence in the course of their duty invariably prioritised the 'need to know' and rarely 'dared to share', which of course maintained secrecy but limited the utility of the data.

Security marking and classification systems

GSC is the official administrative scheme for the sharing of information by all public authorities. The scheme is premised on the principle that all government-related data (including police data) has intrinsic value and requires some level of protection. The sensitivity of information (in terms of the likely impact of its compromise, loss or misuse) is indicated by its labelling with one of three classifications (Figure 5.3) (Cabinet Office, 2013).

Each classification describes a minimum set of security controls that should provide appropriate protection against typical known threats. The significance of each label is that it carries certain caveats on how the information should be stored and transmitted, who should be allowed access to it, and the circumstances in which access is allowed.

Figure 5.3: Security classifications

OFFICIAL	SECRET	TOP SECRET
The majority of information that is created or processed by the public sector. This includes routine business operations and services, some of which could have damaging consequences if lost, stolen or published in the media, but are not to a heightened threat profile.	Very sensitive information that justifies heightened protective measures to defend against determined and highly capable threat actors. For example, where copromise could seriously damage military capabilities, international relations or the investigation of serious organised crime.	HMG's most sensitive information requiring the highest levels of protection from the most serious threats. For example, where compromise couls cause widespread loss of life or else threaten the security or economic wellbeing of the country or friendly nations.

Source: Cabinet Office, 2013 p.4

So, for example, NIM knowledge products are classed as official, CHIS material always is considered secret and interception material falls into the top secret category. While official documents may be circulated (albeit under cover) by post, top secret material is communicated only under strictly controlled circumstances to individuals who have been vetted at a high level and patently need to know it.

Summary

Central to police efforts to process and validate their information is the NIM, now overhauled and seen by many in the police service as a driver for the professionalisation of intelligence work. In large part, the success of this revamped model still depends on inspired individuals and more will need to be done to convince the wider service of its utility. In principle, the police have the mechanisms they need to manage intelligence effectively and ethically, but this analysis very much describes an ideal. Whether staff are sufficiently skilled and motivated to apply these processes effectively and ethically remains moot. Certainly, the recent research into the use of the 5x5x5 system suggested widespread ignorance of even the most basic intelligence practices, so it is to be hoped that its replacement will be accompanied by adequate and appropriate training for the staff who will use it.

Notes

[1] As discussed in Chapter One, the cycle is no more than a useful heuristic and does not adequately represent the reality of the work.

[2] In 2003, school caretaker Ian Huntley was convicted of the murder of 10 year old schoolchildren Holly Wells and Jessica Chapman. Huntley would not have secured employment at the girls' school if the police had carried out the required background checks on his criminal history and character properly. Police failings were examined in a public inquiry led by Sir Michael Bichard.

[3] See Chapter Seven for a more detailed analysis.

[4] CPIA was amended by the Criminal Justice Act 2003, which introduced an amalgamated test for disclosure of material and also introduced a new code of practice.

[5] In *R vs Johnson*, the court laid down minimum evidential requirements that must be satisfied.

[6] An excellent summary of the PII provisions can be found at www.inbrief.co.uk/police/public-interest-immunity.htm

[7] Pillar argues that 'when we lack interest, any epistemic attitude or lack therefore will be as good as any other' (2009 p.415).

8   Full details of the new system can be found at www.app.college.police.uk/app-content/intelligence-management/intelligence-report

9   The research was carried out as part of the NIM review in which the author participated.

Further reading

Billingsley, R (2009), *Covert Human Intelligence Sources: The 'Unlovely' Face of Police Work*. Hook, Hampshire: Waterside Press.

Chainey, S and Ratcliffe, J (2005), *GIS and Crime Mapping*. London: Wiley.

Harper WR & Harris DH (1975), Application of link analysis to police intelligence. *Human Factors* 17, pp.157-64.

Herman, M (2001), *Intelligence Services in the Information Age: Theory and Practice*. New York, NY: Frank Cass.

James, A (2013), *Examining intelligence-led policing*. Basingstoke: Palgrave Macmillan.

SIX

Directing
intelligence work

Introduction

To be truly effective, intelligence work needs direction so that collection supports priorities and provides decision makers with evidence-based assessments of their environments, warnings of new threats that may be just over the operational horizon and support for their strategic priorities or other pressing needs. Direction ensures that scarce resources are not otherwise dissipated outside of priorities on targets of opportunity, on personal crusades, or as a means of adding a gloss to performance management data. Maintaining that focus requires wise and committed leadership, faith in the intelligence process, and the will to be evidence- rather than opinion- or event-led – as experience has shown, by no means a given. Too often those qualities have been lacking in the policing mainstream. Limiting factors have been a slavish adherence to traditional practice and a professional culture that invariably prioritises action over reflection and parochial self-interest over partnership and consilience.

Directing collection

It is axiomatic that there should be clear water between the intelligence officer and the policy or decision maker, but it has been argued that 'although the personnel can be segregated, the functions cannot.... Analysis and decision are interactive rather than sequential processes' (Betts, 1978, pp.66-7). Resolving the kinds of conflicts that arise at that nexus point is far easier said than done. The consequences of fudge or muddle can be far-reaching (see Butler, 2004), so it is easy to see why some might prefer the clarity of the linear model even if it does not quite reflect the reality of that interaction as well as some might imagine. In evidence to the Chilcot inquiry into the intelligence case for the Iraq war, MI6 officers revealed that in compiling their intelligence analyses, the organisation had been 'too eager to please' its political masters and that it had indulged in 'wishful thinking' (cited in

Rollington, 2013, p.128), which suggests that (even though the stakes were very high indeed, or perhaps even because they were so high) their assessments fell far short of that evidence-based ideal. In his evidence to the inquiry, Sir David Omand pointed to an innate tension between the policymaking approach and the analysts' or academic approach to intelligence.[1] In his view, policymakers want to 'shape the world to match … [their] demands', while academics try to 'impose structure on the facts to assemble them and to draw hypotheses from them', a process that tends to end with the policymaker declaring, 'That's all very well, but just try harder.' (Omand, 2010, pp.9-10).

In policing, beyond the specialist headquarters squads and national and regional units whose continued existence is said to be predicated on their ability to convert intelligence into action and demonstrable outcomes (but also continues the long-standing police tradition of 'forming a squad' whenever a new threat emerges), there is only limited understanding of intelligence practice and a propensity to underestimate the merits of the work. As many researchers have found, intelligence often is ancillary to the main business of policing – a kind of parallel universe, co-existing with the 'real' world but not influencing the latter in a meaningful way. In an era of budget cutting, there is an obvious need for forces to become smarter so that increasingly scarce resources are used in more efficient ways. The evidence suggests that investment largely is being made in technology and software rather than in the people expected to work in this digital world.

Intelligence officers should make recommendations for action on the basis of a balance of probabilities. Ideally, they should not shirk from expressing honestly held opinions even if such views may be unpalatable to decision makers. Their analyses should be evidence-based and they must resist pressure to confirm pre-existing biases or to support political imperatives.[2] One commentator noted that 'except by invitation, intelligence officers are voyeurs, sometimes interlocutors, rather than participants by right' (Herman, 2001, p.15). Whether there can ever be a 'correct' distance between intelligence officer and customer is moot. As evidence to the Chilcot inquiry showed, too small a distance increases the former's vulnerability to political pressure; too wide a gap, however, may lead the customer to look elsewhere for their information. It is important that intelligence officers are allowed intellectual independence and that they work within structures that actually promote and value that. That should apply just as much in the policing milieu.

Collection planning

Traditionally, the police used collection plans to coordinate their information-collection activity. In principle, collection planning is a focused, systematic way of meeting intelligence requirements through the tasking of resources that enable the organisation to find, filter and fuse relevant information on a pre-determined issue or problem. In principle, this was a straightforward (if sometimes protracted) task, but in practice one that often was complicated by the fact that intelligence requirements themselves were poorly framed and even less well articulated.[3] Arguably, policing and social problems rarely are well enough understood by the organisation to allow it to assess its priorities in sufficiently meaningful ways, and the expansion of the policing mission (through the neighbourhood policing programme and the like) only adds to the confusion. Consequently, collection was unfocused and, other than on a case-by-case basis, intelligence rarely directed the operational effort. Rudderless, police officers collected information on everyone and everything they encountered, with the pieces variously added to different silos of different intelligence systems so inadequate that they were barely worthy of the name. In part, that is an almost inevitable consequence of the largely reactive style of policing in the UK, a style in which intelligence is a kind of by-product of other, putatively more important, activities.

In the modern era, policing has become adept at responding to events or (despite police chiefs' oft-repeated claims of operational independence) to politically driven imperatives (Tony Blair's campaign against street crime in Britain in 2002 provides a very good example of the latter), with the result that the work effectively was side-lined.[4] At the strategic level, intelligence staffs' duties largely were restricted to servicing the police's ever-increasing appetite for data, while at the operational level their efforts continued to be policy- or case-led rather than intelligence-led (the new policing mantra in modernity), focused on targets of opportunity or on the completion of analytical products to support prosecutions, or, in too many cases, simply on compliance. Only rarely were staff used to prepare the evidence-based assessments of threat, risk and harm that rhetoric suggested were core to their work (James, 2013).

One of the central aims of NIM was to reverse that trend: to provide an evidence base for action; to deliver the direction that previously was lacking; to better articulate intelligence requirements; and to hold commanders to account for fulfilling them. For all the organisational energy expended on it, NIM remains a work in progress. It is to be hoped that the recent overhaul of the model simplifies the task. Today, evidence-based priority setting should be achievable, thanks to the NIM review, to other recent developments in police intelligence work and to decisions taken by central government in the name of police reform.

National security as a local concern

Following the formation of the coalition government in 2010, the Home Office announced its national security strategy in which it identified 15 generic priority risks to the UK (Home Office, 2010). These are separated into three tiers:

- **Tier 1:** international or Irish terrorism; a cyber-attack on the UK; international military crises; major accidents or natural hazards.
- **Tier 2:** an attack on the UK or its overseas territories involving chemical, biological, radiological or nuclear weapons; the risk of major instability anywhere in the world that could threaten the UK; a significant increase in organised crime; an attack on the UK's satellites by another state.
- **Tier 3:** a large-scale conventional military attack on the UK by another state; a significant increase in the threat to the UK from terrorism, organised crime, illegal immigrants and illicit goods; the disruption of energy supplies to the UK; a significant release of radioactive material from a civil nuclear site within the UK; a conventional attack by a state on a NATO or EU member; an attack on a UK overseas territory; disruption to international supplies of resources essential to the UK.

The strategy is notable because it represents the first time these threats, and the need for intelligence about them, has been articulated explicitly by a UK government, even if those risks and requirements could have been inferred. The government's stated aim was to align the operational and intelligence responses of the armed forces, intelligence services and the police to those threats and thereafter to ensure that focus was maintained until such time as each threat was eliminated or until some other, more pressing, problem emerged.

Understandably, given its title, the strategy places a heavy emphasis on national security and on the work of the armed forces and SIAs, which, along with the 'higher policing' units (such as CTC and the NCA), might be expected to lead the preventative, investigative and intelligence efforts in that area. There also is an important role for police forces, which through their local intelligence systems provide the foundations of the whole intelligence edifice. They have a presence in almost every geographically defined community in the UK and can get significantly more 'boots on the ground' than other agencies to collect information about terrorism and other criminal activity that threatens the state, its citizens or their interests. Moreover (in partnership with the other emergency services, local authorities and so on), they are the first responders to any major accidents or natural disasters.

Tackling organised crime

Organised crime is not solely a domestic concern. Globalisation has opened up an almost infinite variety of opportunities for professional criminals and facilitated the emergence and development of criminal networks that now closely resemble transnational corporations. For Williams, these groups are 'transnational organisations *par excellence*' (1994, p.321). He has argued that they present particular challenges to nation states because they 'operate outside the existing structures of authority and power in world politics and have developed sophisticated strategies for circumventing law enforcement in individual states and in the global community of states' (Williams, 1994, p.321). Insidiously, that influence has been spread through local communities by networks' local representatives, who invariably find ready markets for their goods. It also must be recognised, however, that assessing the extent to which this is a case of demand encouraging supply rather than the obvious alternative is tantamount to attempting to resolve the question 'Which came first: the chicken or the egg?'

It would be remiss not to acknowledge that some individuals and communities value that kind of entrepreneurialism highly. They may be active participants, eventually taking their place in the supply chain. They may be opportunistic, taking a share of the profits for themselves whenever circumstances allow (for example, by purchasing wholesale quantities of drugs to sell to friends and family or by supplying otherwise licit services or expertise to criminals). Either way, they may accept the violence, intimidation and corruption that often accompany the business as inevitable by-products of profit-driven criminality. That violence often spills over into law-abiding communities, sometimes with the most tragic results (such as the deaths by shooting of teenagers Charlene Ellis and Letisha Shakespeare in Birmingham in 2003 and of the schoolboy Rhys Jones in Liverpool in 2008 – in both cases the victims were caught in crossfire between rival gangs).

In 2011, the Home Office announced a new strategy to combat organised crime. *Local to Global: Reducing the Risk from Organised Crime* (Home Office, 2011a) was said to be the means by which the Home Office would 'galvanise and coordinate the work of all those with a role in combating organised crime', setting for those agencies 'common objectives and ... a clear line of accountability' (Home Office, 2011a, p.3). Effective intelligence work allows the police not only to gather information about criminality in the communities it serves from those communities, but also to extend their reach, enabling them to identify and accurately interpret the threat from transnational criminal networks. The latter often are controlled from far beyond these shores and they increasingly exploit the virtual world to avoid police interest. In that context, justice will be denied if the police do not have the capability to identify networks' local agents and capture the detail of communications between them and their criminal associates anywhere in the world.

Beyond the high-profile events that are a staple of news media, organised crime has dangerously corrosive effects on communities. It attracts incomers seeking to exploit existing criminal markets or to establish new ones. Often, it is not the plague visited on innocent communities by committed and wicked 'others', as it has so often been portrayed, but a largely disorganised (often chaotic) profit-driven activity that, even when directed by outsiders, seeks (and usually finds) willing collaborators, both as foot soldiers and as customers, within communities. In the process, it may set neighbour against neighbour as relationships are reconfigured by the money, power and influence that involvement in criminal businesses can bring.

Identifying the true nature of a market is critical to formulating effective strategies to dismantle it. For example, it would be a waste of time and valuable resources deploying test purchase officers in a closed drugs market.[5] Equally, specialist knowledge (of, for example, drugs, firearms or explosives) may be required by undercover operatives seeking to purchase illicit commodities. It follows that they would need foreknowledge of the commodities on offer to ensure that they were prepared for the challenge. Tackling organised crime requires strategies that meet the threat from dangerous 'others' and also that recognise, and can ameliorate, its diverse impacts in communities. It is unlikely that the police will succeed on either front without good intelligence.

Setting priorities

In 2013, the coalition government replaced the short-lived national detective agency SOCA with NCA. A significant part of NCA's remit is to present 'an authoritative annual assessment of the impact of and threat to the UK from serious and organised crime and an authoritative assessment of threats to border security' (NCA, 2014, p.2). In other words, it seeks to assess and analyse the threats to the UK as well as to highlight to others the need to collect information about the kinds of criminal organisations described in the previous section. In its *UK National Strategic Assessment of Serious and Organised Crime 2014*, NCA assessed the greatest threats in that context to be child sexual exploitation and abuse, the criminal use of firearms, cybercrime, drugs, economic crime, organised acquisitive crime, organised immigration crime and human trafficking, and preventing those convicted of organised crime from continuing their careers in prison (NCA, 2014).

NIM requires each police force to set an intelligence requirement that describes its own intelligence needs, directs the efforts of its intelligence staff and acts as an *aide mémoire* for its patrol officers and other public-facing staff about the kinds of information they should collect. Even if experience has shown that that imperative has not always been properly understood in every regard, simple logic should dictate that force intelligence requirements also reflect national priorities and that forces should do all that circumstances allow to contribute to tackling them.[6] It follows that they also should have in place arrangements for passing anything they collect related to terrorism, organised crime or those other national priorities to those who might need it, in a secure and timely fashion. Forces are well placed to collect information about those subjects from offenders and from communities, particularly from victims of or witnesses to those crimes.

No policing activity takes place in a vacuum. There is fierce competition for increasingly scarce resources. Demand invariably outweighs supply; balancing the two, a difficult task in itself, has only become more difficult in this age of austerity for the UK's public services. Although there has been little evidence of it since their introduction, there remains the potential for conflict between PCCs, whose concerns primarily are for local issues and the delivery of local policing services, and national bodies like NCA, which for perfectly understandable reasons see the world through a different lens. This is a very old struggle that goes back to the establishment of regional crime squads (RCSs) in the 1960s. Eventually, the regional squads were merged into the National Crime Squad (which eventually morphed into the NCA), but that left operational and intelligence gaps at the regional level that are only now being filled by regional organised crime units (ROCUs). A common complaint about the RCSs was that their gaze was always focused upwards so that regional offices largely prioritised national and international investigations and neglected their responsibilities to provide support to forces and other agencies in their area. Only time will tell if the new units will fall into that trap, but the ritualistic focus on performance and results (the more spectacular the better) certainly increases the pressure to follow that path.

Directing action

The intelligence officer–decision maker nexus has attracted a great deal of attention and interest. Sherman Kent, the guiding light of US intelligence work, observed that there was no single element of the business that was more important than 'the proper relationship between intelligence itself and the people who use its products' (cited in Rollington, 2013, p.124). Nevertheless, that view repeatedly seems to have been ignored in the policing milieu. Essentially, intelligence staff have operated in bubbles, preparing intelligence products that have had little meaningful impact on practice (James, 2013).

Those kinds of experience have been shared by many other researchers. One study found that it was 'all too easy for analytical effort to focus on performance and patterns rather than intelligence development and interpretation', which should be central to police intelligence work (MacVean and Harfield, 2008, p.95). Another highlighted the disparity in the perceived usefulness of analyses generated by police officer analysts and police staff analysts (Cope, 2004).[7] Police staff were seen as less able and their analytical products as less credible. Significantly, managers often bypassed analysts and to all intents and purposes disregarded their analyses, preferring instead to rely on their own experience and on own their professional judgement of events (Cope, 2004). Sometimes, decision makers consider themselves the 'best' intelligence officer and that too can be problematic (see, for example, Jervis, 2011). While this is a noteworthy issue, other explanations are just as worthy of consideration.

Pragmatic realities

Arguably, pragmatism supplies the philosophical underpinning for the 'what works' agenda that dominates research and policymaking in the world of public policing today, even if those behind the movement rarely have acknowledged it. The term is derived from the Greek word pragma, meaning action. It was introduced into the canon of philosophical theory in the US by Charles Peirce, in two articles entitled 'The fixation of belief' (1877) and 'How to make our ideas clear' (1878). Peirce argued that beliefs were no more than rules for action, and that it was the conduct it produced rather than the belief itself that was of sole significance (cited in James, 1904). Put another way, Peirce believed that truth could be measured only by its practical value – something was true only to the extent that it worked or was useful –although as Durkheim (one of the architects of modern sociology and a noted critic of pragmatism) has observed, judgements about utility essentially are context-specific and subjective (Durkheim and Alcock, 1983).

Theorists who inspired pragmatist philosophy included Sir Francis Bacon (1561-1626), philosopher, parliamentarian and jurist (and, incidentally, the acknowledged father of the scientific method), who in the context of this study coined the extremely apposite phrase 'knowledge is power'. Analysts also would do well to heed Bacon's sage advice that 'If a man will begin with certainties, he shall end in doubts; but if he will be content to begin with doubts he shall end in certainties' (Bacon, 1605 p.5/8). Niccolò Machiavelli (1469-1527), a diplomat, courtier and politician and another source of inspiration for the early pragmatists (whose name will forever be linked with duplicity, cynicism and pragmatic morality), is acknowledged as the first to concede that a ruler may need to do immoral things in order to achieve their goals. This is a controversial and contested position even today, but one that has become something of a mantra for the SIAs and for policing.

In common usage, pragmatism has come to be associated with strong leadership and with real-world practice. Usually, it is explained as the ability to act rather than spend time thinking or theorising about acting. Policing needs effective intelligence systems (with all that entails in terms of the infringements of citizens' privacy and human rights) to help officers prevent and detect crime, maintain security and manage risk effectively enough to keep communities safe. That often requires decision makers to rank priorities and sometimes to base decisions on subjective assessments of the greater good or the 'least harm' (see Williamson and Bagshaw, 2001). It has been argued that pragmatic leaders are those who 'accept situations that may not make everyone perfectly happy but that will mostly solve a given situation' (Vessey, 2010, p.193). In the policing milieu, those decisions also must be lawful and ethical and it must be admitted that, in some situations, unconstrained pragmatism can encourage the use of dubious means that present a 'genuine moral dilemma' for the individual and for the organisation (Klockars, 1980, p.33).

Researchers have argued that proficiency within a particular field has a positive impact on a person's ability to make accurate decisions (see, for example, Hammond, 2000). It is often said that experienced people make the best decisions and that seems completely logical, but there is a growing body of research that suggests that experience is only a factor in tasks that cannot easily be broken down into their component parts (see, for example, Dane et al, 2012). Durkheim too has challenged that truism as deterministic. He argued that judgement and experience were little more than personal constructs of charismatic leaders (Durkheim and Alcock, 1983). He attacked pragmatism as anti-intellectual, observing *inter alia* that:

> Just as experience varies with individuals, so does its extent. The person who possesses the widest and best-organised experience is in a better position to see what is really useful. Gradually, his authority here imposes itself and attracts the commendation of others. But is that a decisive argument? Since all experience and all judgements are essentially personal matters, the experience of others is valid for them, but not for me. (Durkheim and Alcock, 1983, p.1)

In the policy context, pragmatism has been described as 'a reasonable and logical way of doing things or of thinking about problems that is based on dealing with specific situations, instead of on ideas and theories' (Harford, 2011, p.1). In action-oriented policing, it is the vehicle by which red tape and other bureaucratic blockers are negotiated to resolve problems quickly with the minimum of fuss. Policing celebrates that behaviour because it is consistent with the dominant organisational 'can-do' culture. Reason and logic often take a back seat to action and existential problems invariably are worked through in mechanistic, process-driven ways no matter what the context.

The police's adoption of a single National Decision Model (NDM) may, as the service claims, help staff to 'make decisions and ... provide a framework in which decisions can be examined and challenged' (CoP, 2014a, p.1), but the model does not recognise the interplay of the experiential, psychological and emotional dimensions of decision making in sufficiently meaningful ways. Divested of that complexity, it perpetuates the fiction that decision makers are consistent, rational and unfeeling. The model may comfort the police organisation that its staff will act, lawfully, ethically and appropriately, but it is questionable whether it offers its employees the reassurance they need that their decisions later will be understood in their proper, human, context.

Expert intuition

In the context of decision making and expert intuition, the heuristics and biases paradigm was advanced in the 1970s by Tversky and Kahneman, who argued that under conditions of uncertainty, people use heuristic devices that 'are highly economical and usually effective but lead to predictable errors' (Tversky and Kahneman, 1974, p.1131). Further work by Tversky, Kahneman and others, quickly led researchers to understand how decisions were *not* taken, that is to say that decision makers 'relied on heuristic as opposed to algorithmic strategies and they rarely employed systematic evaluation techniques' as one might expect (Klein, 2008, p.456).

In 1989, the first naturalistic decision making (NcDM) conference was held in Dayton, Ohio. NcDM aims to explain how decision making works in complex, uncertain environments. Many of the 30 delegates invited were funded by the US Army Research Institute. Sponsors of further research into NcDM have included the US Navy and Air Force and the US National Aeronautical and Space Administration (Schraagen et al, 2008), which demonstrates the 'official' support for the model. After the conference, Lipshitz described nine NcDM models that had been developed in parallel by the delegates (Lipshitz, cited in Klein, 2008). Reflecting on that narrative, Klein noted significantly that:

> People were using prior experience to rapidly categorize situations ... relying on some kind of synthesis of their experience – call it a schema or a prototype or a category – to make these judgments. The categories suggested appropriate courses of action. The static notion of decisions as gambles, which portrays people as passively awaiting the outcomes of their bets, did not fit leaders who were actively trying to shape events. (Klein, 2008, p.457)

Within 10 years of the conference, 'experiential models were accepted as the standard account of decision making by most practitioners' (Klein, 2008, p.457). Kahneman distilled 40 years of research into NcDM to explain the ways that people employ heuristics and biases to make judgements on their realities. He argued that expert judgements simply are the product of experiential learning (Kahneman, 2011).

He drew on labels long used in psychology to describe two types of thinking: system 1, which is intuitive, 'operates automatically and quickly, with little or no effort and no sense of voluntary control', and system 2, which is deliberative, 'allocates attention to the effortful mental activities that demand it' (Kahneman, 2011, pp.20-1).[8] System 1 skills are innate, while system 2 skills demand attention and can be disrupted when that is drawn elsewhere. Although both systems run automatically, system 2 is activated when an event occurs that cannot be managed intuitively. For example, a surveillance officer deployed in the early hours of the morning to observe a suspect's home to record comings and goings, quickly will settle into system 1 thinking and remain in that state until the suspect leaves the property, at which time they switch into system 2 mode to record the suspect's movements, demeanour and so on as a means of assessing the suspect's plans and formulating their own plan of action.

The defining feature of system 2 is that it requires 'effort and acts of self-control in which the intuitions of System 1 are overcome' (Kahneman, 2011, p.31). He argues that 'laziness is built deep into our nature' and that 'a general 'law of least effort' applies to cognitive exertion just as it does to the physical variety (Kahneman, 2011, p.35). Confronted with a mental problem, the lazy (in the relative rather than the pejorative sense) seek intuitive system 1 answers, while the more intellectual reject easy answers in favour of system 2 explanations. Kahneman argues that a 'general limitation of the human mind is its imperfect ability to reconstruct past states of knowledge, or beliefs that have changed' (Kahneman, 2011, p.202). Once someone adopts a new view of their lived reality, they find it difficult to recall former beliefs. The result may be narrative fallacy or confabulation, a 'tidying-up' of past events and an over-confidence in the accuracy of their sequencing and causation. Closely associated with this concept are confirmation and hindsight bias, stereotyping and the halo effect. Each can skew the assessment of intelligence and decisions making. They also are barriers to auditing that action – to determining exactly how decisions were arrived at – which, of course, is often of the utmost importance to managers and certainly (in this context) to courts.

The maxim 'No plan of operations extends with any certainty beyond the first contact with the main hostile force', usually (in a fine example of system 1 thinking) abridged to 'No plan survives first contact with the enemy', has been attributed to Field Marshall, Count Helmuth Karl Bernhard Graf von Moltke (1800-91) (Hughes and Bell, 1995, p.92). In this context, the phrase implies that police professionals on the ground often have to act quickly, instinctively and pragmatically (that is, display system 1 thinking). In conflict situations, they may act in ways that do not conform to the expectations of their managers. However, when they construct their reports (applying system 2 thinking), they often do so in ways that meet the standards required by their managers (and in this case by law or regulation) even if they do not accurately describe exactly what they actually did. Confabulation is one reason for that behaviour but so too is the blame culture that is part of modern policing (see Waring, 2011). Decisions can be challenged or reassessed as part of judicial proceedings long after the events in which they were made. It is largely for that reason that the phrase 'professionals write things down' has entered the police intelligence lexicon, but although that advice may be sound in principle (it may be all that one reasonably can expect), there is a huge body of literature in the field of psychology that suggests that even a written record may no more represent 'the truth' than any other account of the same events (see, for example, Westera et al, 2014).

Napoleon's glance

Napoleon is considered to be one of the greatest strategists and commanders in history. Much of his success is attributed to his expert strategy and his personal bravery. He also was renowned for having the most efficient intelligence and counter-intelligence systems of his era, 'devoting considerable attention to the acquisition of intelligence' (Rosello, 1991, p.103). He used intelligence to disperse the fog of war and counter-intelligence to conceal his true intentions from his enemies. Both were of vital importance to him, but key to his success was his ability to act decisively in the heat and confusion of battle.

The term 'Napoleon's glance' or, to give it its original title, *coup d'oeil* (literal translation: a stroke of the eye – a glance), was coined by von Clausewitz (1788-1831). Defeated in battle by Napoleon, in 1810 he joined the faculty of the new Prussian War College in Berlin where largely he spent the rest of his life trying to unravel the secrets of his adversary's genius (Duggan, 2004). He learned that Napoleon studied the great generals of the past and imitated their tactics, but adapted them for the particular situations he faced. It was the cognitive schemas that Napoleon constructed from this research that were crucial to his success in battle. Von Clausewitz identified the heuristic device *coup d'oeil* as central to the Little Corporal's achievements.

Napoleon believed that *coup d'oeil* was a gift of nature and he valued highly those commanders who displayed it. Von Clausewitz described it thus:

It is, therefore, not only the physical, but more frequently the mental eye which is meant in *coup d'oeil*.... If we strip this conception of that which the expression has given it of the over-figurative and restricted, then it amounts simply to the rapid discovery of a truth which to the ordinary mind is either not visible at all or only becomes so after long examination and reflection. (Von Clausewitz, 1874, Chapter 3)

Von Clausewitz explained resolution, another critical determinant of success as:

An act of courage ... in the face of responsibility.... We have assigned to resolution the office of removing the torments of doubt, and the dangers of delay, when there are no sufficient motives for guidance and presence of mind as denoting, very fitly the readiness and rapidity of the help rendered by the mind. (Von Clausewitz, 1874, Chapter 3)

These four qualities together then – *coup d'oeil,* knowledge of history, resolution and presence of mind – were the key elements of Napoleon's strategy and the foundation stones of his greatest accomplishments (Duggan, 2004). History has not devalued his successes. Indeed, Napoleon's strategies are acclaimed around the world today. In April 2012, Chairman of the US Joint Chiefs of Staff, General Martin Dempsey 'wrote of an "inner eye" and referenced Clausewitz's definition of *coup d'oeil'* (cited in Kirk, 2013, p.5), although the wish is not always carried through into action. Despite that support from a senior military commander, 'much of the [military] education and training continues to be rooted in developing analytical rather than intuitive skills' (Kirk, 2013, p.10). That is in part the consequence of the US's unending quest for information superiority (Kirk, 2013).

Influences on decision makers

Today, the heuristics, experiential learning and schemas that were central to Napoleon's strategies (even if he would not have recognised those labels) have just as much utility in explaining the realities of existential decision making in complex situations. Another dimension to this debate is provided by Tost and colleagues (2011). Citing a wide range of experiment-based research, they argue that individuals' receptivity to advice is influenced by the character of the task to which the advice refers, the character of the adviser, and the decision maker's psychological or emotional state (Tost et al, 2011). The second factor is perhaps the most interesting in the context of the intelligence officer–decision maker nexus. Highlighting the effect of that imbalance, Tost and colleagues argue that 'the more powerful' can 'be less open to using advice from others … [and] can lead individuals to discount advice even from individuals who have high levels of expertise' (2011, pp.53–4). It has been argued that a significant factor in that context is credibility, which exists 'when the product is seen as relevant, timely, expert, objective, and informed; … [moreover] with credibility comes impact' (Peterson, 2003, p.51).

That imbalance in policing has created and maintains a gulf between the intelligence and operational worlds, which is defined by perceptions of their relative worth to the organisation (Innes et al, 2005). Although the police have employed intelligence analysts for many years, the role is perceived as low status and ancillary to the policing mission (Cope, 2004; James, 2013). The limited opportunities available to analysts and the role's relatively low pay (compared with similar roles in the private sector) have resulted in a constant churn of staff, with experienced analysts constantly leaving the organisation to be replaced by (essentially) trainees. Inevitably, novices' views carry less weight than those of their more experienced colleagues and they can more easily be discounted by decision makers.

As many researchers have observed, the divide between the reflective intelligence and the action-oriented operational worlds is rooted in police organisational culture. That divide between 'management cops' and 'street cops' was first documented by Reuss-Ianni (1982). She argued that their 'incongruent value systems' generated a classic management versus workers dynamic (Reuss-Ianni, 1982, p.5), with the former valuing 'pre-planned and packaged solutions' and the latter prioritising 'immediate local police responses' to social problems (Reuss-Ianni, 1982, p.7). Reuss-Ianni's research led her to conclude that it was the street cop culture that determined the 'day to day practices of policing' (1982, p.7).

It is, at least in part, that cultural conditioning that encourages police decision makers invariably to see the world in binary terms and to respond with pragmatism, *coup d'oeil,* or stage 1 thinking. Self-evidently, experience and expertise are critically important in any organisation. Kleinig (1996, p.2) argues that judgment based on experience is the critical factor in decision making in the policing context. Moreover, Napoleon's successes demonstrate that in fluid, dynamic, often dangerous situations those qualities can be the difference between success and failure. They are, and should be, prized, but those kinds of situations do not represent the norm in public policing. They represent only a fraction of police business. When time allows, deliberation – in controlled environments, shown to benefit experts and the less skilled alike (Moseley et al, 2012) – should always be part of the process. Finally, it is worth observing that policing often seems to be in crisis; pragmatism is never valued more highly than it is in a crisis. Time spent in calm reflection on that correlation would not be time wasted.

Summary

Direction is of crucial importance in intelligence work. The police receive strategic direction from the Home Office, which recently has fixed strategic priorities for them and the other agencies of social control. In principle, the police should now be able to set more focused as well as more comprehensive intelligence requirements that prioritise the collection of information around identified priorities (of both the national and local variety). That should develop more accurate intelligence pictures and provide the data that decision makers need to be truly evidence-led, but the faith that the institution's decision makers have in intelligence, in the intelligence process and in their intelligence staff remains questionable. Organisational culture is a significant feature in that regard, but the evidence suggests that pragmatism and the inclination to act (real positives in policing) may often replace reflection and consilience. A more thorough analysis of decision making in this context is needed.

Notes

[1]   Former head of GCHQ.

[2]   Perhaps the best example can be found in the Butler review. (Butler, 2004)

[3]   Not the least significant factor was that attempts to coordinate law enforcement activity at the national level (first through the formation of NCS and NCIS, then through their merging into SOCA) had only partially succeeded in delivering that holistic picture of crime in the UK.

[4]   Policing found setting priorities particularly difficult during Tony Blair's first two terms in office. Tonry recorded 33 'tough on crime' government initiatives between June 2001 and May 2003 alone, and 13 crime summits between 1999 and 2003 (cited in Reiner, 2007).

5   In this context, an open market is one in which there are few barriers to access. Suppliers will sell to anyone who appears to have the means to buy. A closed market is one in which sellers will only deal with people they know or who are 'referenced' by a trusted individual.

6   This is one of the key issues addressed in the Home Office's strategic policing requirement.

7   Once it was common to find officers employed in the role, but that rarely is the case today.

8   The terms were coined in the 1870s by the pragmatist philosopher William James.

Further reading

Heuer, R (1999), *Psychology of Intelligence Analysis*. Washington, DC: Central Intelligence Agency.

Home Office (2010), *National security strategy - a strong Britain in an age of uncertainty*. London: Home Office.

Kahneman, D (2011), *Thinking fast and slow*. New York, NY: Penguin.

Klein, G (2008), Naturalistic decision making. *Human Factors*, Vol. 50, No. 3, June pp.456–60.

Jervis, R (2011), Why Intelligence and Policymakers Clash. *Political Science Quarterly*, Volume 125, Number 2, summer.

NCA (2014), *UK National Strategic Assessment of Serious and Organised Crime 2014*. London: NCA

SEVEN

Opportunities and threats in the digital age

Introduction

In 2014, IBM – a global brand and one of the biggest names in computing – estimated that 90% of the world's data had been created in the previous two years, and that 80% of that was unstructured (Dennis, 2014). Structured data is data held in fixed fields within files. Unstructured data comprises images, audio, video, emails and data from monitoring devices of all kinds. In the policing context, it might include the content of witness statements or officers' notes of evidence. Technological limitations have meant that institutions have struggled to make sense of unstructured data as whole. It is argued that the internet is a key medium for democracy and protest, and is changing the relationship between governments and citizens (RUSI, 2015, p.6). If the environment is changing and the police now have the capability to use data in more intelligent ways, to what extent does that represent a variation of the social contract? Citizens may be concerned about the exploitation of technologies and 'big data' by the police for reasons that go beyond the financial or other intrinsic costs. Police legitimacy constantly is in flux, waxing and waning as police successes are celebrated or their failures condemned. The use of these massive datasets raises significant ethical issues, not least in the way that it may threaten traditional freedoms. Big data's links to data-driven, predictive policing (PP) – the 'next big thing' in the fight against crime – also are worthy of examination, as is the case for the use of social media intelligence (or SOCMINT as it has been termed). Arguably, its wider use is desirable not only because of its intelligence dividend, but also because it may result in lesser use of potentially more intrusive intelligence methods.

Big data

There is broad agreement that Western society has moved into the big data age (see, for example, Simon, 2013). Big data is an evolving, though some would say still nebulous term, that describes vast amounts (usually exabytes) of data, whether in structured, semi-structured or unstructured form or in any combination of the three. Users currently are generating in excess of an exabyte of data every day. The rate of data generation is growing exponentially, but the term does not just describe the vastness of the data available. It implies that hitherto unrealisable benefits may emerge if the correct tools can be found and used. Using data analytics, big data can be mined to deliver information that has intrinsic value. A significant characteristic of the big data debate is the number of questions (in proportion to the number of answers) the debate generates. It seems that even industry experts are yet to come to terms with what it means for businesses and for wider society.

Origins of the term

Elliott argues that the term 'big data' is so vague it has allowed many to claim the distinction of coining it, but it probably should be attributed to Doug Laney of Gartner Research (2013). In 2001, Laney posited that big data was characterised by the three Vs: volume (traditional storage methods are inadequate), velocity (churn exceeds normal data processing speed) and variety (non-uniform data). While many others have sought to explain the term, those explanations largely represent no more than elaborations of Laney's original definition (Elliott, 2013, p.1). There is broad agreement on the worth of analysing big data and a confidence in the ability of data analytics to find patterns in previously disparate data: essentially needles will be found no matter no matter how big the haystack or how many haystacks there are.

Huge relational databases existed for many years before the term surfaced. Examples in policing are the Police National Database (PND) and the DNA Database. Elliott (2013) has argued that a label was needed for the new technologies that were emerging at the beginning of the 21st century and developers eventually settled on big data. Those technologies were Apache Hadoop and other non-tabular databases. Hadoop is an open source software project that enables the distributed processing of large datasets across clusters of servers. It has been called 'the world's *de facto* Big Data platform' (GigaOM, cited in Simon, 2013, p.114). Hadoop is extremely flexible and can handle many different kinds of data. It is used by dozens of household-name, information-dependent companies such as Facebook, Yahoo, Google and Twitter. In 2012, there were 35 billion devices connected to the internet and more than a trillion devices were network-enabled (Kahler, 2012). These devices generate a huge amount of data. In an era when the cost of data storage continues to fall rapidly, these numbers are probably much higher today. Knowledge is power; it is also a generator of wealth. It has been argued that big data often is a term 'thrown around by people with something to sell' (Harford, 2014, p.1). That is hardly surprising, given that many businesses (not least those named here) have proved adept at monetising the raw data or, through the use of analytics and data visualisation, at identifying patterns in data and, to their great financial advantage, packaging it for sale to others.

Veracity of big data

The notion that institutions can exploit the use of those 35+ billion devices operating in the world or can develop meaningful intelligence from the vast quantities of digital information they produce are attractive propositions for police commanders, but just how much reliance should be placed on that data? As Chapter Five showed, whether intelligence has value or is actionable in the policing context largely depends on its provenance – on a *post hoc* assessment of its reliability and trustworthiness. The ability to find value in previously unusable data or to combine data from different databases and sources, and to present it in ways that allow for new insights into behaviour, may offer the police advantage, but the provenance of big data is just as important as that of any other information the police may contemplate using.

In that context, IBM's introduction of 'veracity' into its big data modelling criteria should act as a red flag for the policing institution.[1] IBM's research suggested that poor data quality cost the US economy in excess of $3 trillion in 2013 (IBM, 2013). Veracity in this context relates not just to data that is incomplete or inaccurate, but also to data uncertainty; some data is inherently unpredictable. The police need to exercise due caution in extrapolating meaning from it and must have in place systems and processes that *inter alia* assess its reliability and trustworthiness. The numbers involved are huge. In 2010, the US Library of Congress decided to archive every public Twitter tweet; by January 2013, the archive contained around 170 billion tweets (Joh, 2015). In just one second, roughly 2.5 million emails (67% of which are spam) are sent; about 50,000 Google searches are made; 9,600 tweets are broadcast; and in excess of 40,000 Facebook postings made (Internet Live Stats, 2015). That implies that if the police are to make sense of it, they will need to make significant investments in their own IT infrastructure, sub-contract the work to trusted partners, or forge new relationships with IT companies.

An analysis of Twitter traffic provides an interesting example of the challenges analysts face in making sense of the kind of data that falls under the heading of big data. In August 2014, Twitter, in a US Securities and Exchange Commission filing, reported that about 8.5% or 23 million of its 271 million active users were in reality automated accounts, or 'bots', programmed to broadcast tweets at specified times or in response to particular events; a further 5% of its traffic was spam (Crum, 2014). Motti (2014) has highlighted that though some bots are harmless, they can mislead those seeking to make sense of data. Moreover, spam bots reproduce more noise in the system and are of little meaningful use to anyone.

Other Twitter-related data that has the potential to mislead is a fake user account, created either as a way of inflating the number of followers of a celebrity account (as a means of establishing or marketing the celebrity's fame) or to facilitate the broadcasting of spam. There is a link between the two, a correlation between the number of account followers and the amount of spam sent to that account. Therefore, it is no surprise to learn that 71% (that is, around 13.5 million) of US President Barack Obama's Twitter followers do not actually exist (Greathouse, 2012). It may be an obvious fact, but nonetheless a fact worth stating, that as the data mountain grows, so too does the volume of unreliable data in existence. That only increases the challenge of accurately assessing its provenance.

Policing with big data

Big data offers many possibilities in the law enforcement arena, but, as the previous sub-section implies, one of the most significant challenges that the police face is differentiating between good and bad data when so much of it is system or user-generated (with, in the case of the latter, few quality control or other filter measures at the point of production). It is argued that the most significant questions for public institutions revolve around that cost–benefit nexus point (boyd and Crawford, 2012). Broader questions of capability, capacity and legitimacy also are important in this context. It confidently can be asserted that in the UK, police and other law enforcement and SIAs routinely collect vast amounts of data in the ordinary course of their work preventing and detecting crime or collecting intelligence. It seems highly likely that big data will provide new insights into criminal activity and enable the police to use increasingly scarce resources more efficiently, but there is not yet the evidence to support the contention that it is 'being used by [UK] police forces to identify locations more likely to experience crime' (POST, 2014, p.1).

POST highlighted the national DNA database, the IDENT1 fingerprint database and the PND as big data sources, but accepting these as representative of the term would be something of a stretch for most experts in the field (2014). Rather, these are examples of structured databases that long have been capable of producing knowledge for policing purposes. Even though they hold large amounts of data, they do not fit most accepted definitions of big data. Elliott has argued that one of the great difficulties in making sense of the phenomenon is the way in which the term is used to 'rebaptize projects possible using previous technology ... in a fairly blatant attempt to jump on the Big Data bandwagon' (2013). For all the big data = big brother-type connotations of the phenomenon, that desire to associate one's efforts with the label reflects an aspirational 'brave new world' dimension that individuals and institutions seem keen to tap into. POST's misidentification of PND and so on as big data lends weight to Elliott's case. It also demonstrates the widespread confusion around the term.

That confusion is not only evident in the UK. For example, in 2012, it was reported that the success of a city police department in Texas in making more efficient use of its relatively scarce human resources could be attributed to the harnessing of big data (Fogarty, 2012). In fact, the data used to inform the reorganisation of the city's patrol and beat boundaries comprised highly structured emergency-call records. Even though more than one million records were analysed, that does not equate to big data; the records – and, in principle, the technology necessary for their analysis – always were available. The fact that in 2012 the Hardoop technology was used to make sense of that pre-existing data does not, except at the level of rhetoric, necessarily imbue it with greater significance. Police have used such data to identify crime patterns and hotspots for many years, but it was never labelled 'big'.

Similar methods have been employed in many US cities, including Los Angeles, California; Santa Cruz, California; and Atlanta, Georgia. Equally, while they all have earned the praise of local police chiefs and community leaders, (from this distance) it seems that their successes have relied more on effective interpretations of structured data rather than on the big data revolution. There are notable exceptions, which suggests that as the technologies mature and as the police come to understand them better, forces may get nearer to exploiting their potential. For example, in New York city, the New York Police Department has collaborated with Microsoft to deliver a 'domain awareness system'. The system 'links information from sources like CCTVs, license plate readers, radiation sensors, and informational databases' to reduce crime (Joh, 2015, p.35). Nowhere in the UK is the pressure to embrace these kinds of technologies greater than in the metropolis. In 2013, a report by the London Assembly Budget and Performance Committee (LABPC) roundly criticised the MPS for spending a significant portion of its budget on outdated technology (LABP, 2013).

The response from the force was swift (at least in policy terms where the wheels usually turn very slowly). In February 2014, it announced a four-year total technology strategy, with the goal of enabling the MPS to 'become the first truly digital police force' (MPS, 2014, p.3). The strategy includes a number of aims; in the context of this section, the most interesting relate to its plans for greater use of analytics in its systems. In year 1, the force aims to 'integrate more of the MPS intelligence systems to provide a source for future analytics ... including a POLE (Person Object Location Event) data store ... and a platform for storing a variety of media sources', and in year 2 to 'enhance the POLE data store to support big data analytics' (MPS, 2014, p.15). This all comes at a significant cost to Londoners. In a written response to the LABP, a senior officer forecast that the investment needed to support the strategy was 'significantly more than the average £70m/annum invested on technology in the force' from 2010/11 to 2012/13 (Rowley, 2013, p.3).

Data: quality versus quantity

Lack of information may not be the 'principal obstacle to accurate intelligence judgments' (Heuer, 1999, p.51). Richards Heuer argues that there may be circumstances in which additional information can contribute to more accurate analysis, but that is not a given; there also are circumstances in which extra information, particularly contradictory information, may confuse rather than clarify understanding (Heuer, 1999). In his seminal work, *The Psychology of Intelligence Analysis*, Heuer recounted various experiments with experts (including horseracing handicappers, doctors and clinical psychologists) as test subjects. In each case, the aim of the experiment was to understand the relationship between the amount of information used to make a judgement and its accuracy (Heuer, 1999).

In the betting on the horses experiment, eight experienced handicappers were given a list of 88 variables found on a typical race record, for example 'weight to be carried; the percentage of races in which horse finished first, second, or third during the previous year; the jockey's record; and the number of days since the horse's last race' (Heuer, 1999, p.53). Each handicapper was then given sanitised data for 40 races and asked to use the five pieces of information they considered the most significant to rank the top five horses in each race. The experiment was repeated using 10, then 20, and finally 40 of what each considered the most salient pieces of data. When predictions were compared with race outcomes, it was found on average that accuracy remained the same regardless of how much data was used. However, each handicapper expressed steadily increasing confidence in their judgments as more data was used. In other words, their predictions were no more accurate for using 40 pieces of information than for five, but the more data used, the more confident they felt in their predictions. Heuer concluded that it was the handicapper's mental model, 'their knowledge and assumptions as to which variables are most important and how they are interrelated', that was the critical factor, not the amount of knowledge they collected (1999, p.58).

In a similar vein, Kirk questions whether, given the almost infinite amount of data that increasingly is available to planners and researchers, any organisation can process this information well enough 'to provide decision makers with the right amount at the right moment so they may be able to make the best choice' (Kirk, 2013, p.84). He argues that, in the modern era, the appetite for more and more information can never be satisfied and that too much organisational energy is expended on confirming what already may be known. A serving US Army officer, Kirk's argument is based on a study of his own environment; a similar theme was identified in UK policing (see James, 2013). Commanders took comfort from collecting data and analytical products as shields to be deployed when they needed to deflect criticism from outsiders.

Given that Kirk's analysis is in the context of combat and military command, one should be careful about implying a direct read-across to the policing milieu, but his findings very much mirror Heuer's analysis. Kirk argues *inter alia* that the:

> ... pursuit of information-superiority creates decision paralysis ... creates a risk-averse culture because leaders require more data to make a decision in order to avoid backlash ... stifles both creative and critical thinking because it produces an overreliance on the analysis of facts and data rather than emphasizing new or reflective ideas ... and most dangerously, it produces the false belief that the fog of war can be removed. (2013, p.85)

The juxtaposition of these arguments allows for easy identification of points of comparison. It is interesting just how much agreement there is between the two when Heuer's findings were based on experiments in the 1970s and 1980s and Kirk's on a qualitative assessment of his professional environment today.[2] The studies suggest that the correlation between volumes of data and the meanings that may be inferred from them is weak, or at least that the relationship between the two is not linear, as some advocates of Big Data would have us believe.

Predictive policing

There is an obvious symbiosis between big data and the state's great new hope for reducing crime, namely predictive policing (PP), defined by HMIC as the 'methods used by police forces to use and analyse data on past crimes to predict future patterns of crime and vulnerable areas' (HMIC, 2014b, pp.72-3). The police have used geographic information to map crime for more than 20 years. Much of the innovation in the field was driven by the US Mapping and Analysis for Public Safety programme (Chainey and Ratcliffe, 2005).

The PP concept

From relatively humble beginnings (initially Geographic Information Systems [GISs] were lauded for their descriptive rather than their predictive qualities – even if the latter sometimes could be inferred), in one of its latest iterations it is claimed to be a technology that can 'predict highest risk times and places for future crimes ... targeting place-based prediction areas, depicted in 500 feet by 500 feet boxes on maps, that are automatically generated for each shift of each day' (PredPol, 2015). That is quite some leap. The police have been identifying crime 'hotspots' for many years and, arguably, there is only so much value in a map once crimes have been plotted, so it is worth asking the question, 'What really has changed in the period to imbue today's crime maps with such predictive power?'

Chainey and Ratcliffe suggest that the early systems development of GISs has given way to a putatively more scientific development of the field – the development of 'analytical methodologies, techniques and processes for the advancement of spatial understanding' (2005, p.3). For police forces across the developed world under huge pressure to deliver more with less, these new methodologies seem to have been greeted with the kind of appreciation more usually seen in desperate situations involving drowning people and lifebelts. That is understandable in an era when police professionalism has come under such heavy scrutiny and there seems almost constant political pressure on forces to ensure that their policies are evidence-based and consistent with what has been perceived to work in other spaces and places. The police's never-ending search for silver bullets has taken them, in this case, to IT providers only too keen to assist them in this endeavour. Many UK forces, including the MPS, Kent and Greater Manchester, have trialled or have even adopted predictive technologies.

Examining PP's claims

There is surprisingly little research evidence into PP on which scholars and policymakers can rely; none was identified in the UK policing context. The findings of those studies that have been conducted largely have been equivocal. For example, in 2012, an evaluation of a PP crime reduction initiative in Shreveport, Louisiana (the Shreveport Predictive Policing Experiment) did not find a statistically significant reduction in property crime and there was insufficient evidence to determine whether the model's predictions could generate greater crime reductions over traditional crime-mapping methods. Positives were that officers perceived benefits from the initiative; that the initiative may have represented a more efficient use of resources; and that in some circumstances it improved community relations (Hunt et al, 2014).

Notably, Perry and colleagues (2013) reviewed the literature on PP tools, compiled case studies of US police departments employing the software, and proposed a PP taxonomy. The researchers concluded that there were four categories of PP, namely:

- methods for predicting crimes: ... approaches used to forecast places and times with an increased risk of crime;
- methods for predicting offenders: [that] ... identify individuals at risk of offending in the future;
- methods for predicting perpetrators' identities: ... used to create profiles that ... match likely offenders with specific past crimes;
- methods for predicting victims of crime: ... used to identify groups or, in some cases, individuals who are likely to become victims of crime. (Perry et al, 2013, p.1)

This review of PP concluded that for it to be effective there needed to be synergy between the analytical and investigative efforts. Researchers found that successful interventions typically had 'top-level support, sufficient resources, automated systems to provide needed information, and assigned personnel with both the freedom to resolve crime problems and accountability for doing so' (Perry et al, 2013, p.1). As much as these methods may use innovative programs to crunch bigger datasets than human analysts easily could process, when stripped of the jargon and techno-speak that are characteristic of these kinds of initiatives these all are very basic procedures that always have been characteristic of effective and efficient investigations. There is little here that is actually new. As the researchers identify, making predictions is only half the job; the other half is actually carrying out meaningful interventions (Perry et al, 2013). There is plenty of evidence in the UK to support that argument. One of the most significant factors in the failure of the UK's NCIS (the first iteration of a national intelligence agency) was that it had no operational arm. One of the fundamental failings of NIM was that it increased the divide between the intelligence and operational worlds rather than encouraging synergy between them.

While PP may have promise, in the light of this analysis it is difficult to escape the conclusions that its merits have been overstated and that the police have unrealistic expectations of it. In the UK context, some successes (notably in Kent and West Yorkshire) have been reported, but it has been argued that more independent research is needed to determine its real value (POST, 2014). More evidence is needed to satisfy objective observers that PP is worth pursuing in its current form and is not just an example of the triumph of hyperbole and marketing over substance. Further research should include fundamental questions about the necessity and appropriateness of the technologies currently employed and the extent to which the criminal environment rather than the actors within it should be the subject of such detailed inquiry. On the basis of this study, it seems that there is a need for a more rigorous analysis of both the benefits and the costs of PP. The former may well outweigh the latter, but currently it is difficult to dissent from the view that 'Many agencies may find simple heuristics sufficient for their predictive policing needs' (Perry et al, 2013, p.1).

Social media

Founded in 2004, 2006 and 2010 respectively, Facebook, Twitter and Instagram have revolutionised the way that people, particularly younger people, communicate.[3] In 2014, somewhere between 30 and 33 million people in the UK used Facebook, the premier social networking site for almost all UK adults online (Rose McGrory, 2015).

Trending inexorably upwards, user numbers will continue to rise for the foreseeable future. The rapid proliferation of social media presents the double-edged sword of opportunity and challenge to the state's institutions, not just in the context of law enforcement, but also in many other environments (such as health, where, in the context of the vaccination debate, it has contributed to interactions between medical companies and the public as well as providing opponents with new means of organising their opposition – see Wilson and Keelan, 2013). Even though many websites allow for a degree of user customisation, they are not included in most definitions of social media. Instead, the term describes a variety of different applications, including social networking sites (such as Twitter and Facebook), virtual worlds (such as World of Warcraft), wikis, blogs and video-sharing sites (such as YouTube) (Kaplan and Haenlein, 2010). Taylor (2012) posited that social media may be broken down into four categories – social networks, content-sharing sites, content-ranking tools and geo-locations tools – each with their own particular characteristics and therefore each presenting measurably different threats and opportunities. Social media is perhaps best explained as the utilisation of these platforms to create, challenge, revise and share ideas and online content in ways that represent collective user experiences.

Threats presented by social media

There are a number of challenges to investigating offences committed via these media, relating primarily to practice and legislation (or in some circumstances, the absence of legislation). In terms of practice, the internet knows no physical boundaries so there are obvious challenges in cases where the offending user is outside the UK and offenders have not been slow to exploit those opportunities. Effective communication with transnational policing bodies (including Europol and Interpol, discussed in Chapter Three) is essential, as it is with authorities in the US where many of the servers through which this data is transmitted are sited.

Offences commonly committed via social media can be prosecuted under UK legislation such as the Public Order Act 1986, the Malicious Communications Act 1988, the Protection from Harassment Act 1997 and the Communications Act 2003. The Director of Public Prosecutions has issued guidelines to prosecutors dealing with crimes committed on social media (DPP, 2014). Essentially, prosecutors have been directed to prosecute robustly communications that include credible threats of violence or damage, those that might constitute harassment or stalking, or any offence involving a contempt of court. However, within the guidelines there is an obvious attempt to balance this with the right to freedom of expression (a right protected by Common Law and by Article 10 ECHR) and perhaps a less obvious attempt to ensure that the judicial system is not overburdened with cases that are better dealt with in other ways.

Many myths have emerged about the evils of social media. It might be imagined that it can allow ill-intentioned users to create new identities for themselves to facilitate wrongdoing, but a recent study found that it was 'remarkable how little deception people attempt on social media platforms. Apart from a little embellishment on dating websites, most people are still relatively cautious about presenting a false image of themselves and most use social media simply as an online extension of their offline selves' (Taylor, 2012, p.4). Equally, there was speculation that social media was a factor in the riots of 2011 that began in London and then spread across the UK, that it was used by the rioters to mobilise their forces and to organise looting activity. Research has shown that in fact 'Facebook and Twitter were not used in any significant way by rioters' (Lewis et al, 2011). In contrast, they were used extensively by those involved in the clean-up operation, with researchers finding that messages on the subject reached more than seven million users (Lewis et al, 2011).[4] Interestingly, users seem to have fewer concerns about the government monitoring their data than the media companies themselves:

> Whereas 60% were very or fairly concerned about social media websites such as Facebook monitoring and collecting information about their online activity, and 55% had the same concerns about search engines such as Google, only 46% and 43% had the same concerns about the US and UK Governments respectively. (TNS BMRB, cited in Anderson, 2015, p.33)

Opportunities presented by social media

Social media is utilised by police forces as a new way of connecting with the public. Almost every force has corporate Facebook and Twitter accounts and the same media are used extensively for official purposes by various staff members. They offer the potential for greater engagement with a different demographic and with traditionally hard-to-reach groups (Police Foundation, 2014). They also may help forces to better understand social problems and enable them to respond to community concerns in more effective ways, but research has shown that social media cannot just be bolted on to existing communications arrangements. They have 'their own logic, norms and culture' that police need to understand and respect if they want to maximise their potential (Davis et al, 2014, p.7). Equally, it should be understood that there are consistencies. For example, the Pareto principle seems to apply to the use of social media just as it does to the problem of crime.[5]

Users freely share many details of their lives online. It is no surprise that the police and other agencies should want to harness such a ready source of information. Sir David Omand, former head of GCHQ, was one of three researchers who coined the term SOCMINT as a label for the intelligence dividend from the use of social media (Omand et al, 2012). They argue that SOCMINT offers opportunities for improving public security through crowdsourcing information, new opportunities for research and understanding, near-real time situational awareness (a real boon in intelligence practice), better insight into groups and better forecasting of criminal events. The researchers recognise, however, that public acceptability of SOCMINT's use by law enforcement and citizens' understanding of its proportionality and necessity are as important as they are for any form of intelligence collection (Omand et al, 2o12, p.2).

With 20% of users willing to accept unknown Facebook friend requests and around one in three deceived into thinking they are communicating with a human when instead messages routinely are machine-generated (Taylor, 2013), the police have not found it difficult to utilise this new source. It is to be hoped that the police evaluate the data they collect in the same way as other sources; data provenance is no less important. The police do not have *carte blanche* to access social media for investigative purposes. Lawful collection depends on the application of the same human rights principles that underpin other investigative techniques.

This may not be well enough understood by some in the institution. There is evidence that law enforcement agencies are repeatedly accessing social media in ways that breach the spirit, if not the letter, of RIPA (CSC, 2015). Acknowledging the now widespread use of social media, the CSC cautioned those who seek to exploit these media for law enforcement purposes that their endeavours should not be considered a replacement for traditional practices. The CSC's comments signal that practitioners' actions in this context are being scrutinised, although there remain substantial questions over the effectiveness of that scrutiny. Some have argued that RIPA's inadequacy means that practitioners are not supported well enough and that there is an urgent need for new legislation in this area (Omand et al, 2012; Anderson, 2015; RUSI, 2015). Certainly, law enforcement's use of social media as an investigative tool in what amounts to a legislative vacuum challenges traditional conceptions of police legitimacy and appropriateness.

Summary

Big data inevitably will have an impact on policing and intelligence practice just as it will on every other aspect of the social world. There is evidence that many states, including the UK, have undertaken (and still are undertaking) the mass screening of data for the purposes of national security with all that entails for citizens' rights. There is no evidence that the police have done the same, although there clearly is an aspiration to use big data tools and techniques to help the organisation discern meaning from previously meaningless data. The evidence for PP's merits has been overstated and much more research into the techniques employed is required. There are no easy solutions to the problem of crime. Police commanders should be sceptical of statements that suggest otherwise. Currently, it may be argued that social media provides policing with far more opportunities than threats but there is need for regulation of police activity in this context in the causes of individuals' privacy and of investigative certainty. The temptation to replace traditional practice with (cheaper) desk-bound investigations is huge. In some cases, the latter may be appropriate, but cost-cutting measures should be undertaken in this area only with the greatest of care.

Notes

1. Laney argues that extra Vs add only unnecessary complexity and that veracity is something that he addressed in the volume element of his definition. As his many posts testify, he is a staunch defender of his 3Vs definition, but that has not prevented any number of efforts to reinvent that particular wheel.

2. As a student of the US Naval War College, it is highly likely that Kirk would have been exposed to Heuer's scholarship.

3. Other platforms exist, but these three seem the most popular.

4. The free messaging service available on BlackBerry phones, known as BBM, was used extensively by rioters, but strictly that does not fall under the heading of social media.

5   After the Italian economist Vilfredo Pareto, who observed that 80% of Italian income was shared by 20% of the population. The principle is that most results in any given situation are determined by a minority of causes. Thus a small proportion of social media users generate a disproportionately large amount of the traffic; a small number of motivated offenders commit a large proportion of recorded crime.

Further reading

Omand, D; Bartlett, D; Miller, C (2012), Introducing Social Media Intelligence (SOCMINT). *Intelligence and National Security* Vol. 27, Iss. 6.

Perry, WL; McInnis, B; Price, CC; Smith, SS; Hollywood, J (2013), *Predictive Policing: The Role of Crime Forecasting in Law Enforcement Operations*. Santa Monica, CA: RAND Corporation.

Police Foundation (2014), *Police use of social media*. London: Police Foundation.

Simon, P (2013), *Business Case for BIG DATA*. Hoboken, NJ: Wiley.

EIGHT

Intelligence failure

Introduction

As was highlighted earlier, much of our understanding of intelligence practice comes not from policing, which largely has hidden this facet of its work from public view, but from SIAs. Such knowledge is derived in particular from the US intelligence community, which for many years has encouraged research into its practices and has endorsed both publication of research findings and scholarly reflection on the themes that have emerged from them (often under the auspices of bodies such as the US National Institute of Justice or the Central Intelligence Agency's Center for the Study of Intelligence). There now is a relatively large body of scholarly research on intelligence failure on which practitioners can draw. There is much less on intelligence success and that is bound to skew the public's perception of the work. That is just as true of policing as it is of the security milieu.

US academic (and national security 'insider') Richard K. Betts and a second US academic (and former US Navy intelligence analyst) Erik J. Dahl persuasively have argued that no matter how many resources the intelligence community is able to call on, no matter how many analytical processes it develops, no matter how much data it collects, crises or calamities – that in the modern era have come to be labelled intelligence 'failures' – are inevitable. Against that background, the following questions are posed: To what extent are those analyses applicable to the UK policing milieu? Does the increasing emphasis on big data obscure the intrinsic value of 'little data' to intelligence success? What efforts are the police making to manage the risks associated with intelligence failure?

Actionable intelligence

The phrase actionable intelligence is a relatively modern creation that links action and intelligence and, intentionally or otherwise (its genesis may have been a calculated act or simply an etymological quirk), invests the product of that association with a utility that neither, on its own, possesses. It implies accurate and timely intelligence, and purposeful and justified action, qualities that always may be present, but, given the ubiquity of the term in the policing milieu (see, for example, HMIC, 2015), it sometimes may not. The focus here is on strategic and tactical intelligence failure. Strategic intelligence addresses long-term goals that are of concern to senior leaders, while tactical intelligence is short term and more likely to be used by frontline officers and staff for planning or managing specific operations.

Strategic intelligence failure

It probably was Betts who first noted that strategic intelligence failures can more often be traced to political or psychological causes than organisational ones.[1] He observed that 'Producers of intelligence have been culprits less often than consumers. Policy perspectives tend to constrain objectivity and authorities often fail to use intelligence properly' (Betts, 1978, p.67). Arguably, nothing that has been learned about police intelligence practice in the 37 years since Betts made that statement comes close to challenging that view.

Figure 8.1: Conceptualising strategic intelligence failure

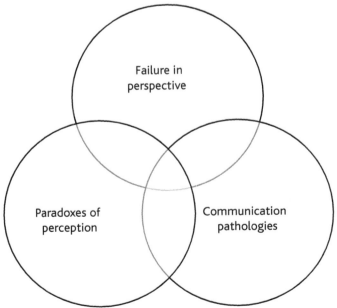

Failure in perspective

Paradoxes of perception

Communication pathologies

Indeed, the genesis of strategies intended to counter terrorism (the CONTEST strategy) and transnational organised crime (the NCA operating model) are, in large part, premised on the limitations of police and SIAs to prevent every manifestation of deviance. Intelligence failure has been conceptualised as an inevitable by-product of one or more institutional failings. Those shortcomings are: failure in perspective; pathologies of communication; and paradoxes of perception (Betts, 1978, p.63) (see Figure 8.1). Each is examined in this section and elaborated on in the context of UK policing.

Failure in perspective

Failure in perspective goes beyond the notions of cognitive consistency or dissonance that usually come to mind when barriers to understanding in this context are considered. This is the idea that 'Particular failures are accorded disproportionate significance ... [when] they are considered in isolation rather than in terms of the general ratio of failures to successes' (Betts, 1978, p.62). The kinds of failings described here are not unique to the armed forces, SIAs or the police, nor are they only to be found in intelligence work. Indeed, they can to be found in many institutions and in many dimensions of practice, but their impact on the social world is likely to be more significant in this, than in many other, contexts because of policing's critical role in protecting citizens and buttressing the power of the state.

Questioning the capability and accountability of institutions that have power over citizens is justified on many levels, but the tendency always is to focus on failure rather than on success. Arguably, that tendency is innate. Evolutionary psychologists posit that individuals today display the same traits that made the survival of early *Homo sapiens* possible. That includes the instinct to seek out news and information about potential threats, the better to prepare their defences. People are hardwired to take more notice of bad news than good. Those who regularly access news media will not need to rely on any scholarly study to recognise the veracity of that statement. In that context, there may be little that intelligence officers, individually, can do to mitigate the criticism that inevitably comes their way whenever a failure is identified. Perhaps the best that can be hoped for is a more nuanced understanding of human frailty even if history has shown that the more usual response is to seek out the culprit and rush to apportion blame.

In recent years, the police and SIAs have been keener to highlight their successes in preventing terrorist incidents and major crimes. In November 2014, MPS Commissioner Bernard Hogan-Howe announced that the force and its SIA partners had prevented five terrorist attacks in 2014 (BBC, 2014). These kinds of announcements are welcome – successes should be celebrated – but, as has been highlighted, 'there are no clear indicators of what the ratio of failure to success in intelligence is, or whether many successes on minor issues should be reassuring in the face of a smaller number of failures on more critical problems' (Betts, 1978, p.62). One terrorist 'spectacular' may outweigh any number of successful interventions by the police and SIAs. Moreover, in that context, it is worth recalling the words of the Irish Republican Army following its failure to assassinate Prime Minister Margaret Thatcher (by bombing the Grand Hotel in Brighton, the venue for the 1984 Conservative Party conference). Infamously, an IRA spokesperson said, 'Today, we were unlucky but remember, we only have to be lucky once: you will have to be lucky always' (cited in Moysey, 2008, pp.270-1). Regardless, this greater willingness to at least talk publicly about operational successes is highly symbolic and represents a positive step towards the kind of openness and transparency that citizens expect of public authorities in modern democracies.

The police do not need to look very far to find an example of the consequences of not getting positive messages across to those they serve. When SOCA was established with a former spymaster at its head, it adopted many of the operating practices of the UK's SIAs. Initially, and characteristically for an SIA, it published very little on its work and seemed actively to shun the news and other media. Arguably, there were good reasons for the agency's conservatism, but one outcome of its approach was that it was unable to respond effectively enough when it came under fire from critics for its perceived lack of success in combating organised crime and in seizing professional criminals' assets (see, for example, HCHASC, 2009). In 2010, some four years after it was established, the agency published its first annual report (SOCA, 2010), which acclaimed some of its greatest successes and explained its work in much more detail than it had managed hitherto. That signalled a significant shift in the agency's communications strategy, but, as subsequent events have shown, the effort was in vain; the damage to SOCA's reputation already had been done. Holed below the waterline, it was only a question of time before it would sink.

Pathologies of communication

The whole process of collecting and evaluating information in a timely fashion, then communicating the results of analysis to decision makers in sufficiently convincing ways, was critically assessed earlier. Most intelligence failures have their roots in that process. The problems of information collection were also discussed earlier. In large part, the police collection effort lacks focus. The placing of a disproportionate value on quantity rather than on quality creates 'noise' in the system – an inability to distinguish between relevant and irrelevant data. This was just the kind of problem identified in the wake of the July 2005 London bombings (ISC, 2006), a problem exacerbated, during the largest terrorist investigation ever carried out jointly by the police and SIAs in the UK, by shortcomings in their strategic capabilities to counter the 'home-grown' terrorist threat (ISC, 2006, p.44) and the inadequacy of the agencies' data retrieval processes (ISC, 2009, p.47). Data evaluation too can be problematic. The use of too strong a filter and useful information will be discarded; too weak and the noise will increase making the task of retrieving valuable data even more difficult.

That the intelligence officer–decision maker nexus is a site of intelligence failure also is well understood. One of the most significant figures in modern security studies, Loch Johnson, characterised 'disregard of objective intelligence by policymakers [as] one of the seven sins of strategic intelligence failure' (cited in Gill and Phythian, 2012, p.149). Policymakers' subjectivity was a significant feature in the assessment of the intelligence case for the Iraq war even if the subsequent association with those events of a 'dodgy dossier' of intelligence (see, for example, Hall, 2013) suggested that the greatest failings lay elsewhere.

Arguably, focusing on the lines of communication within and between agencies as the central problem 'implies that procedural curatives can eliminate the dynamics of error … [for that reason] official post-mortems of intelligence blunders inevitably produce recommendations for reorganisation and changes in operating norms' (Betts, 1978, p.63). That certainly applies in the policing milieu, where the failure of police to communicate effectively enough with partner agencies such as social services, health authorities and so on in the context of child safeguarding frequently has been questioned in public inquiries and reviews of cases where children have died in suspicious circumstances (such as the cases of Baby P, Daniel Pelka and Victoria Climbié). In each of those cases, the resultant inquiry highlighted systemic failings and made a large number of recommendations in respect of information collection and sharing policies and practices. However, an in-depth study of 20 serious case reviews (SCRs) conducted in the period 2009-10 challenged normative expectations of the police and other agencies, and questioned their ability to deliver the improvements in safeguarding that successive case reviews suggested were needed (Brandon et al, 2011).

Reviewers found that expectations of what could be achieved were unrealistic. Inquiry recommendations invariably demanded too much – attempted to reshape practice too radically, too quickly. Despite repeated calls for fewer, smarter recommendations, in the 20 cases selected for in-depth analysis, there was a total of 932 recommendations. That broke down to an average of 47 recommendations per inquiry. The researchers found also that the drive for smarter recommendations only increased the burden on already hard-pressed professionals. Characteristically, most recommendations focused on additional training or new ways of complying with various norms rather than acknowledging the complexities of engaging with hard-to-reach families or finding new ways to promote professional judgement or support reflective practice. This is a common complaint, so it is no surprise to see it made again in these circumstances. The same concerns have been expressed in the context of intelligence analysts' training. It has been observed that what is delivered 'generally means instruction in organisational procedures, methodological techniques, or substantive topics [whereas] more training time should be devoted to the mental act of thinking or analyzing' (Heuer, 1999, p.5). In the UK, the situation remains much the same today.

Highlighting the need for a more holistic analysis of these phenomena, Brandon and colleagues highlighted that:

> The interface between societal issues like deprivation and maltreatment rarely featured in recommendations or action plans ... [and there] was rarely a research evidence base cited for the recommendation made: they tended, instead, to be based on learning from the single case which was assumed to have wider implications. (Brandon et al, 2011, p.47)[2]

The limits on what may be learnt from a single case should be obvious. Certainly, they are demonstrated in the difficulties that successive governments have experienced in their dealings with ECtHR over the UK's covert policing powers. Betts would not have been at all familiar with the SCR process, but the substance of his argument also can be applied to this phenomenon. He argues that even substantial changes in communications processes may be insufficient and that there are clear limits to the improvement of the intelligence milieu because of factors beyond the control of intelligence staff.

The belief that crises and calamities can be avoided 'by perfecting norms and procedures for analysis and argumentation … is "illusory" … intelligence can be improved [only] marginally' (Betts, 1978, p.61). The external pressures on policing policymakers to do something – anything – in the face of a perceived crisis can be huge; promises to undertake significant structural change or 'grand plans' to 'beat' crimes such as burglary (Operation Bumblebee), robbery (the Safer Streets initiative) or sex trafficking (Operation Pentameter) often are the result; NIM was unusual in that it represented both a commitment to structural change *and* a grand plan to reduce crime across the board by 10% within two years, which some may feel strained credulity given the history of policing in the UK (James, 2013). Policymakers' overconfidence in wide-ranging systemic reform largely is unmerited. Ultimately, the effect of any administrative change is limited because of the almost infinite number of variables influencing an organisation's work. Structures and systems are important, but so too are things over which, at least in the short term, managers have little control (such as organisational culture, staff morale, the ever-changing social and political contexts within which the institutions operate and so on).

Paradoxes of perception

Organisational changes aimed at alleviating one or more intelligence pathologies may create new pathologies or revive old ones. For example, 'making warning systems more sensitive reduces the risk of surprise, but increases the number of false alarms, which in turn reduces sensitivity' (Betts, 1978, p.63). It is inevitable that policymakers and intelligence officers will see the world through different lenses; the latter are unconstrained by the pressures that accompany decision making. For Betts, the most significant pathology in this context is the linkage of analysis (or lack thereof) with strategic decisions, which he identifies as falling within one of three categories relevant to the military or national security spheres: attack warning; operational evaluation; and defence planning (Betts, 1978 p.62). They are equally applicable in the policing milieu.

Attack warning refers not only to forewarning of an enemy's immediate intentions, but also to the quality of the advocacy needed to convince decision makers to take action in response. There is ample evidence of that dialectic in policing (see, for example, Gill, 2000 and Cope, 2004). Operational evaluation refers to the need to constantly monitor operations to assess progress and to ensure that necessary changes in strategy or tactics are made in a timely fashion.

An intelligence failure may result from failing to adapt to changing circumstances. In principle, policing can rely on one of the nine standard analytical products, the operational intelligence assessment (OIA), for that purpose. In practice, few such products are completed, and reporting instead is carried out informally or as part of the T&C process. That side-lining of an intelligence norm is more a symbol of policing's operational–intelligence divide than of intelligence failure. Indeed, no failures worthy of the name were revealed by this study, but it is noted that an OIA is produced by intelligence staff independently of decision makers whereas assessments made in T&C forums may be skewed by any number of factors.

Defence planning alludes to the estimation of the long-term threats posed by enemies. In the policing context, that estimate is captured in a strategic assessment prepared by the intelligence staff and presented to commanders at a strategic T&C meeting. The segregation of intelligence and policy is determined in these meetings. Policy is captured in the control strategy – long-term priorities that will attract the bulk of available resources. Intelligence failure sometimes is the product of inadequate planning. In a perfect world, there should be less scope for failure in this setting, but that assumes that the decision maker has determined those priorities on the basis of accurate intelligence and was not swayed by other factors, and that there are no significant changes in the operating environment before new plans are made. The social world is far from ideal and leaders' plans often may be blown off course, may founder or may even be wrecked by what the Tory patrician Harold MacMillan is said to have described as 'Events dear boy, events.'

Tactical intelligence failure

In the policing milieu, the number of tactical intelligence failures that has come to public attention in recent years far outweighs the number of strategic failures. On the one hand, that may be because the former are far more visible, but, on the other, the challenge of identifying strategic failure is much greater because, *inter alia*, strategy often describes long-term aspirations rather than goals, no matter what the official rhetoric implies. Strategy may fail for any number of reasons, but a few are linked to intelligence. Conversely, tactical failures are much easier to identify, and their causes much simpler to discern, because the consequences are more immediate and much more likely to be exposed to judicial scrutiny or other inquiry. Moreover, they are more obviously damaging to the institution in question and to communities. One commentator has argued that it is impossible to achieve consistent tactical success, that some reverses are inevitable and must be accepted. Therefore, SIAs' performance should be judged by their influence on strategic rather than on tactical outcomes (Gentry, 2010). While that may be no more than another pragmatic reality, it is a difficult argument to sell to communities conditioned to expect the kind of organisational mind-set in their state-appointed guardians implied by labels like 'total policing' or any of the myriad other putatively public confidence-building epithets (not least 'to protect and serve') used by the police.

The concept of surprise attack

Dahl argues that intelligence professionals and policymakers must 'recognise that the ultimate goal of their plans is to prevent surprise' (2013, p.21). Surprise commonly is perceived as a means of gaining tactical advantage. For Betts, it is 'a force multiplier ... [that can] keep the victim reeling when his plans dictate that he should be reacting' (1982, p.5). Warnings of strategic failure appear frequently (see, for example, Williams, 2015). Usually they are so vague that they may prompt a recalibration of the national threat level but otherwise have little influence on policymakers and are of limited practical use in preventing attacks. That is because 'surprise attacks', even when they have strategic-level consequences, are 'tactical events involving relatively few decision-makers and occurring in a relatively confined space and time' (Dahl, 2013, p.22). A general warning of trouble ahead is insufficient. Decision makers need to know the 'when, where, who and how?'.

Echoing Betts' analysis of the causes of intelligence failure, Dahl observes that 'precise intelligence and receptive policymakers' are required to prevent surprise attacks (2013, p.24). He argues that it is not better strategic intelligence analysis that is needed, but better tactical intelligence collection practices. Dahl argues that although analysis is important, the most significant determinant of future success is the collection of information precise enough to deliver effective tactical responses and that requires a different dynamic – one that is closer to the action (2013). That argument certainly applies in policing, where, for example, analytics may identify a drug-trafficking network, its hierarchy, its theatre of operations and so on, but at the point when a decision is made to target the network's operations (or alternatively to continue to monitor the network or to move on to other priorities), investigators will be heavily influenced by the kind of precise data that usually can only be obtained from, for example, a well-placed informer (that is, dates and times of drug shipments, transportation arrangements, concealment methods and suchlike).

Surprise attack in the UK

Earlier, the author highlighted the paucity of literature on intelligence successes, of which there have been many, and the barriers to understanding when one's view of institutions' work is so skewed. There have been any number of inquiries that have examined the intelligence capabilities of the UK's police and SIAs. Most have lauded the agencies for their skill, courage and tenacity; understandably, few have described their successes to any meaningful extent. The ISC's inquiries into the July 2005 London bombings and into the murder of Fusilier Lee Rigby were more revealing than most. Both vindicated operational decisions not to switch scarce resources away from investigations that had been afforded a higher priority. The ISC's reports on those terrible events are of great value to researchers and practitioners (ISC, 2006; 2009; 2014b). They are readily available online and are not reproduced here. Within them are key messages about the events themselves as well as the challenges the UK's police and SIAs face in countering surprise attacks.

The reports provide unprecedented detail on potential threats to the UK and its citizens. For example, and probably most troublingly, they reveal that there rarely are enough organisational resources to counter all of the potential threats identified. It has long been understood that policing usually is 'playing catch-up' with criminals, as old methods evolve or new forms of deviance (such as cybercrime) emerge. The reports reveal that SIAs are under the same pressures to prioritise the use of their surveillance or other covert assets (so necessary for combating organised crime or terrorism) against those targets that appear to pose the greatest risk of harm. Both, too, must ensure that their activities can be assessed as compliant with citizens' human rights. The reports also highlight that precise intelligence and receptive policymakers play significant roles in pre-empting surprise attack, but even when both are present that will count for nothing if the institution in question does not have the tactical capability to counter the identified threat.

In praise of little data

Much currently is made of the potential value of big data to policing. It seems likely that its impact on the policing institution largely will be positive, but, in the UK context, there is not yet much hard evidence of its worth. Largely ignored in the debate over its utility is the value of little data, which the police have relied on for as long as the institution has existed and which routinely provides tactical advantage. Indeed, without it, policing simply could not operate in anything like its current form. A telephone call to police informing them of a robbery in progress, information from a CHIS about the whereabouts of an escaped felon, a report from a health professional regarding patterns of injury to local children – these all are little data that require, in some cases demand, a tactical response, which if not forthcoming may erode public confidence in the institution and ultimately threaten its legitimacy.

Moreover, it is the little data that the police rely on to get their job done. Thanks to the telephone call, the police can despatch a response vehicle to apprehend the offenders or, at least, to render assistance to the victim, record witnesses' descriptions of the suspects, and so on. The CHIS's information will save resources being wasted on a manhunt in which there are no guarantees of success. The injury data can be assessed in the context of reported crimes to determine the dark figure and to aid the institution to tailor its response more effectively. In the context both of the London bombings and the murder of Fusilier Rigby, the really key choices made in the lead-up to those terrible events were tactical rather than strategic. Ultimately, the intelligence available was sufficient to point to the 'who?' but did not provide the important pieces of little data that were needed, namely, information on the 'when, where, how and why?' that in the ordinary course of events always have persuaded decision makers to switch resources from other pressing needs.

Risk

Thinking about risk requires a redefinition of the social world; people and groups are neither good nor bad, public space is neither welcoming nor threatening. Relative to each other, they simply are more or less risky. It has been argued that in this paradigm 'everyone poses more or less of a risk for everyone else' (Beck, 2009, p.3). There are two basic approaches to risk assessment: the clinical and the actuarial (Kemshall, 2001). Clinical methods are derived from the public health arena; actuarial methods use statistical analytical techniques to predict risk. Both have advantages and disadvantages. The consensus seems to be that the solution is to combine both so that professional knowledge may mitigate the potential impact of statistical fallacies.

In a world of almost infinite threats and finite resources, prioritisation is essential. In the context of modern policing, decisions usually should be based on assessments of threat, harm and risk. It seems obvious that managing risk would be central to police business. It has been claimed that police officers are 'professional risk takers, with risk-taking being at the core of police professionalism' (CoP, 2013c). Traditionally, policing used a five-step process to identify, analyse, evaluate and finally to take action to mitigate the risk. The fifth step is to Remove the risk, Avoid the risk, Reduce the risk or Accept the risk (RARA), although a substantial body of opinion suggests that too often the second, more obviously risk-averse, option is selected (see, for example, Heaton, 2010; Gilmore, 2013).

It is doubtful whether those big philosophical questions are factored into police decision making. As noted in Chapter Six, circumstances often demand immediate action and do not allow individuals time to think or theorise about action (although, as also highlighted, policing is not so action-oriented that that should be the norm). Instead, utilitarianism guides most decisions about risk. That is evident from the risk assessment provision of the police's NDM, a decision model claimed to be 'suitable for all decisions ... [that] should be used by everyone in policing' (CoP, 2014c). The model directs staff to assess the situation, the specific threats, the risk of harm and any potential benefits. Decision makers are advised to 'consider [among other things] the objectives of preventing discrimination, promoting good relations and fostering equal opportunities' (CoP, 2014c), which, as argued earlier, may be far easier said than done.

Strategic management of risk

There are many different sets of risk management standards, several of which are relevant to intelligence work. They include the International Standards Organisation 31000:2009 (risk management), ISO/IEC 17799:2005 (information security) and the EU's CORAS risk management model. Commonly, they recommend processes to help decision makers manage uncertainty. Though there may be small differences in approach, each model describes processes meant to encourage the systematic analysis of situations and events in terms of their probability and their consequences, and the subsequent assessment of control measures. For example, the probability of anyone hacking into the PND is low, but the consequences of such an act could be far-reaching so the physical and technological barriers erected around the PND must reflect that. These kinds of risks usually are managed at the institutional level, although that does not imply that they are set in stone. Risk management is a dynamic process that must reflect changes in the operating environment.

Managing operational risks

Notwithstanding the evidence to the contrary, the CoP has claimed that its approval of 10 risk principles 'is a first step towards the police service encouraging a more positive approach to risk by openly supporting decision makers and building their confidence in taking risks' (CoP, 2013c). The guidance is lengthy; each principle is qualified by what in another context might be described as range statements. It will not be repeated here, but perhaps in the context of this study it is worth considering Principle 8, which states that 'To reduce risk aversion and improve decision making, policing needs a culture that learns from successes as well as failures. Good risk taking should be identified, recognised and shared' (CoP, 2013c). It is to be hoped that practitioners will respond in a positive manner. This analysis has shown that the 'need to know' has always outweighed 'dare to share', and there is a paucity of scholarly literature on police intelligence practice, but executive support for the latter represents a very welcome statement of intent.

Traditionally, the police have used the 3PsLEM model to assess operational risks and/or the PLAICE model to assess risks related to the use of covert methods, the latter being described as more suitable for actions deemed to be secret and in need of special protection (Billingsley, 2009). The abbreviation 3PsLEM, refers to Police and community, Physical, Psychological, Legal, Ethical and Moral risks. The model was developed in the 1980s by John Grieve for the MPS. PLAICE refers to Physical, Legal, organisational Assets, Information, Compromise (to staff, methods and so on) and the Environment. Others have described the utilisation of those processes in some detail.[3] They will not be examined much further here, but it is worth reflecting on the competence of operational police staff to assess dimensions of risk. For example, can a police officer really assess psychological risks? Can the public be confident in the ability of the police to be moral arbiters? How many officers want that responsibility? These are questions that did not seem to have been considered very much, if at all.

Plans are well advanced to introduce Management of Risk in Law Enforcement (MoRiLE), a new risk management model for UK policing that uses a structured methodology that encourages greater consistency in the identification of strategic priorities, to review 12 months' worth of organisational data. It is meant to dovetail with the simplified NIM. The aim is to produce a national picture of risk using the NIM strategic assessment processes. Positives are that the model encourages users to assess risk on the basis of overarching themes, harm criteria, likelihood, legal requirements and the organisational position (whether or not the institution has the capacity and capability to manage the identified threats). There remain references in the new model to moral risks but largely these are concerned with reputational harm to the institution that may be associated with its actions/inaction. There is now no requirement for an assessment of psychological risks, which arguably held those completing assessments as hostages to fortune.

The MoRiLE process fuses clinical and actuarial approaches and in that sense represents risk management best practice, but the calculation of risk depends in each case on subjective assessments of the environment by the lead author so achieving consistency in reporting will be key to real understanding. For the policing institution, the new model does not necessarily represent a paradigm shift in practice. Arguably, risk management will remain a defensive act, one meant to protect the institution and its staff in the event of unforeseen calamity. That is not a criticism of policing; it is simply recognition that for most public institutions, given 'the inherent unpredictability of future behaviour, it is generally accepted that "defensibility" rather than "certainty" is the goal of risk assessment practice. A "defensible" risk assessment is one which is judged to be as accurate as possible and which would stand up to scrutiny if the handling of the case were to be investigated ...' (Robinson, 2003, p.113).

Summary

The evidence suggests that intelligence failure invariably is regrettable, often (but not always) calamitous but completely inevitable. The phenomenon of strategic failure has been attributed to attack warning – the inability to identify a threat or to heed the warning of it; operational evaluation – a consequence of failing to adapt to changing circumstances; or defence planning – where the failure is attributed to poor or inadequate planning. Tactical failures largely can be ascribed to a lack of precise intelligence, unreceptive policymakers, or insufficient tactical resources to allow for timely responses to identified threats. It is little data that invariably answers the 'when, where, and how?' questions that intelligence staff rely on to persuade decision makers to act on their analyses. Effective risk management is a critically important element in averting intelligence failure. The police institution has acknowledged that it needs to take a more positive approach to risk. It also is in the process of introducing a risk management model that combines clinical and actuarial assessments of risk in a manner that has come to be recognised as best practice. However, the institution, and those scrutinising it, also need to recognise that (for any number of different reasons) some risks simply cannot be managed.

Notes

[1] Dr Betts is now Arnold A. Saltzman professor of war and peace studies, political science department, Columbia University; director of the Saltzman Institute of War and Peace Studies; and director of the international security policy programme in the School of International and Public Affairs, Columbia.

[2] That of course was exactly the same policy adopted by successive governments in response to rulings of ECtHR.

[3] See Harfield (2009) and Billingsley (2009).

Further reading

Betts, RK (1978), 'Analysis, War, and Decision: Why Intelligence Failures are Inevitable', *World Politics*, 31:1, pp.61–89

Butler, Lord (2004), *Review of Intelligence on Weapons of Mass Destruction Report of a Committee of Privy Counsellors*. London: HMSO.

Dahl, EJ (2013*), Intelligence and Surprise Attack: Failure and Success from Pearl Harbor to 9/11 and Beyond*. Washington, DC: Georgetown University Press.

ISC (2009), *Could 7/7 Have Been Prevented? Review of the Intelligence on the London Terrorist Attacks on 7 July 2005*. London: HMSO.

ISC (2014), *Report on the intelligence relating to the murder of Fusilier Lee Rigby*. London: HMSO.

NINE

Taking stock: looking ahead

Introduction

Beyond its crime fighting, safeguarding and numerous other responsibilities, the police service is a significant actor in a network of agencies, centres and units that protect the UK, its citizens and its wider interests against an increasingly diverse range of threats. There is nothing very new about that; the institution has taken a leading role in those contexts since its emergence in 1829. Without accurate and timely intelligence, the police simply could not function; there is nothing very novel about that either. Police officers carried out intelligence work from the earliest days of the new police, even if their efforts rarely attracted that label. Formal intelligence-gathering activities have been undertaken since the 1880s, particularly by the Special Branch, which targeted insurgents and radicals. The first criminal intelligence units emerged in the 1950s in response to the increasing mobility of professional criminals after the Second World War.

Thereafter, the police intelligence apparatus developed to confront new threats as they appeared (such as transnational organised crime) to meet legal and political imperatives, or to support the developing network of local, regional and national policing functions. In modernity, external factors invariably have been the most significant drivers of organisational change – the need to respond to the increasing scale, diversity and complexity of threats (many of which originate far beyond the UK's shores), and to the variety of political and legal demands on the institution. Most of those topics already have been addressed, but it is worth taking stock here, to focus on some of the central themes that emerged in the course of that analysis and to consider how intelligence work might develop in the future.

Taking stock

The police service finally has established the classic pyramid-style national intelligence system its leaders always said they wanted (see, for example, Stevens, 2001) but never seemed sufficiently willing to make the investment in. Founded on local intelligence units and with the

NCA at its apex, the system now has the regional element it previously was missing, in the form of the ROCUs and RCTUs (see Figure 9.1).

Figure 9.1: UK police national intelligence system

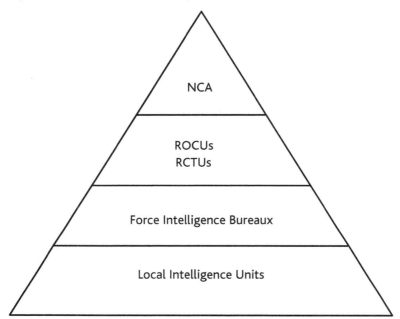

That element is important because it goes some way towards filling the intelligence and tactical vacuums that have existed since the demise of the regional crime squads (RCSs) at the beginning of the century. At this point, a degree of equivocation over the prospects for the system probably is wise. As the next section discusses, it is likely to take some time for the new arrangements to bed in, but in principle the structure provides the true interconnectivity from local to global that previously was lacking. That is to say that the chain from the top of the pyramid to the bottom is now complete. Moreover, the new regional units are not simply reiterations of the RCS model, which exclusively was police owned and operated. Their successors are much more focused on partnership, with embedded GAIN, HMRC, UKBF and NCA staff. In future, blockages in the flows of information between the different agencies will not be so easily explained.

Coordinating practice

As was highlighted in Chapter Three, the NCA is going through its own teething problems, which can only have been compounded by its labelling as 'incompetent' by an Old Bailey judge after a series of blunders and calamities led to the collapse of a £5m fraud trial. Prosecuting counsel was forced to concede that the state of the evidence presented by the agency was 'half investigated, material missing, material misleading' (Syal, 2014).[1] The challenges of bringing together different organisational cultures and working practices are well understood; they are hardly likely to be less less challenging in this case, but the NCA plays a pivotal role in coordinating the investigative effort against transnational organised crime, and that not only increases the pressure on the organisation but also makes the job of resolving the issues more urgent.

The NCA is UK policing's single point of contact with Interpol, Europol and other international and transnational security and policing bodies, and has monopoly control over interception and other most sensitive policing techniques. Coming hard on the heels of SOCA's demise, the failings identified by the court and by its own staff may reveal more about the challenges involved in attempting to mould a single national agency from diverse precursor national and regional bodies than they do about the abilities of the new agency and its staff. Managing change is always difficult; when it is a reorganisation on this scale, it inevitably requires the wholesale relocation and reskilling of staff, adaption to different ways of working, and the shaping of various organisational technologies and cultures into a cohesive whole. Bumps along the road are only to be expected. That is not to suggest that those shortcomings should be accepted; they should not. However, in discussions of public policy, one must always guard against advocating simplistic explanations for what essentially are pretty complex institutional challenges.

Unlike SOCA, the NCA's commitment to NIM and its establishment of national coordination and tasking process that mirrors arrangements in forces and at the regional level should allow the agency to make the best use of its resources in support either of its own investigations or of those conducted by its partners (which includes forces and regional units). Much has been made of the NCA director-general's ability to direct forces to assist the agency, but a more significant factor in the future interoperability of these bodies is the extent to which the NCA is willing to provide assistance to forces when they need it or if (like SOCA) the NCA and regional units largely 'go it alone'. Presumably, that will depend on circumstances – the national threat level and so on. However, a common feature of these arrangements is the way in which the needs of those at the bottom of the pyramid (in this case police forces) are neglected because of the perception that regional or national endeavours are more worthwhile because they are targeted at 'bigger fish'. If these developments are to be seen as a reconfiguration of policing rather than empty rhetoric, managers at every level of the tasking and coordinating process (that is, in LPUs, forces, regions and the NCA) will need to be vigilant to ensure that resources are matched with need. For that reason, tasking decisions should be reviewed regularly to ensure the continuing integrity of the process.

Policing's relationship with the UK's SIAs

The police service occupies a clearly defined place in the UK's national security architecture. SIAs have the power neither to arrest nor detain people; they rely on the police (usually CTC or one of the RCTUs) to take the lead in gathering evidence, making arrests and preventing harm to communities. Of course, in undertaking those duties the police often are reliant on secret intelligence supplied by the SIAs. Routinely, the flow of information from SIAs to the police is now handled by CIUs so that it is firewalled from the wider law enforcement community until a decision can be made about its further dissemination. The information may be used in evidence in criminal trials. Sanitisation is a key element in that process, but there also are other procedures in place for handling intelligence evidence and disclosures to ensure that as far as possible the court is presented with the best evidence.

It seems that the relationship between the police and SIAs (particularly MI5) in the context of CT is a harmonious and productive one; that was a message that came through clearly from respondents in one of the research projects on which this study is based and from the evidence presented to the various inquiries referred to earlier. There can be no question of where the real power in that relationship lies. No matter what rank a police officer achieves, they will never have the same access to the corridors of power as their SIA counterparts, but there is evidence of common purpose in the contexts of security and public protection and (according to police respondents in this study) sufficient checks and balances in the existing system of governance to ensure that significant problems are resolved quickly. In a world of secrets, lies and deception, that may be as much as anyone can reasonably expect.

Individuals concerned in acts of terrorism are also likely to be involved in other, more routine, criminality (such as fraud, money laundering and so on). One issue that has exercised intelligence staffs' minds since police CIUs were first introduced is the extent to which intelligence passed to the police by SIAs that reveals evidence of offending outside of SIAs' remits can be used to support police investigations. The convention is that the originating agency 'owns' the intelligence. Therefore, the CIU may only use it as directed by the originator (traditionally via the 5x5x5 system). Understandably, SIAs are extremely concerned about the possibility that their methodologies, or even the fact that they are interested in a particular individual or group, may leak out. For that reason, even within CIUs, a firewall is established between CT and the rest of the service.[2] *A priori*, despite the advantage that this kind of intelligence could confer in mainstream policing, there does not seem to be very much appetite for change and that recently was confirmed in a little-noticed Home Office-sponsored review of the system, which recommended a continuance of the status quo.

Police–community relations

To many, police intelligence practices, like work and taxes, are a necessary evil. The state questions their use only rarely; the public was once largely ignorant of them, but it is becoming increasingly important that communities are convinced that the necessity for the work outweighs the ills that may befall them as a consequence of it. Intruding into privacy may fundamentally alter police–community relationships in ways that will not necessarily be counterbalanced by the new means of public engagement that the new technologies offer. Reflecting on the NYPD's use of a system capable of linking information from multiple sources, Joh notes that 'The very quality of public life may be different when government watches everyone – surreptitiously – and stores all of the resulting information' (2015, p.61).

As was highlighted in Chapter Two, UK citizens' right to privacy is protected in law; the extent to which they consent to violations of that right is central to our understanding of police legitimacy. Drawing on a number of public surveys undertaken between 2013 and 2014, POST highlighted the limited research on the use of these kinds of data by the UK's police and SIAs. POST reported that 'People seem to be more willing to trade-off personal privacy concerns when data cannot be used to identify and target particular individuals and when they perceive personal or social benefits from the use' (2014, p.4). That may hold true, but in the light of whistleblower Edward Snowden's revelations[3] about the activities of the SIAs, the threshold for citizens' acceptance of that trade may be much higher than some may imagine.

Police pragmatism

There are few certainties in the intelligence milieu. At the strategic level, realistically, often one can do no more than hope for the best while preparing for the worst. Operational intelligence work is equally challenging, but that rarely comes across in public pronouncements. The police institution and its staff routinely underplay the complexity of criminal events and the intricacies of the operational responses they demand. That is professionally and culturally consistent; pragmatism is the dominant characteristic in that environment. Leaders want facts to help them make decisions; courts expect fact-based evidence and are not overly concerned with much else. Policing is a highly symbolic act; its public image is that whatever the pressure, the thin blue line may bend but it will not break.[4] That drives not just a 'can do' but a 'can always do' culture and a utilitarian institutional narrative. Moreover, there always is a need to protect covert methodologies, so (lawful) obfuscation or omission of material that may betray tools or tactics are significant features of file preparation. *Post hoc,* complex situations routinely are stripped of their existential meaning and reduced to sequences of dates, times, places and events to meet organisational imperatives and the demands of legal process, but in intelligence work the fog of war is all around and that is a message that the police should convey much more clearly and much more consistently.

Consider the pressure on you as an intelligence manager when, with a crime in action, you are trying to assess an ever-changing intelligence picture by juggling CHIS, surveillance assets and all manner of other intelligence sources to provide your operational teams with the knowledge they need to accomplish their task. Situational awareness is paramount; you must constantly reappraise events as they unfold; manage the physical and other risks to your colleagues, to the subject and to the communities you serve; and at the same time ensure that your actions are proportionate, legal, accountable (you will need to record every decision and also explain your thought processes in arriving at it) and necessary. Those are not simple tasks – particularly if you have taken on board senior police leaders' advice to be lawfully audacious. Unsurprisingly, then, heuristics abound and pragmatism invariably triumphs over reflection.

Several examples of policing's anti-intellectualism have been presented to support that view. They are not meant as value judgements, simply as comments on the operating environment and the challenges that staff frequently face in their professional lives. Cultural conditioning means that the inclination to act always will be present. Most police managers understand that their failure to choose between 'equally perceived aversive outcomes' (Alison et al, 2015 ,p.295) may be seen as indecision, a label that once attached arguably is more career-threatening the higher one rises in the organisation but is seldom career-enhancing at any level. Of course, the other side of that coin is that 'a few lucky gambles can crown a reckless leader with a halo of prescience and boldness' (Kahneman, 2011, p. 204).

Assessing individuals' claims of success in that context is an inexact science but it is vital that charisma should never be allowed to distort understanding of reality. Marx (1988) argued that decisions should be judged against a utilitarian ideal on their proportionality and on their consequences (both intended and unintended). Sometimes, it may be wholly understandable that pragmatism is preferred to idealism. Even a champion of intelligence like von Clausewitz argued that 'deference to intelligence can frustrate bold initiative and squander crucial opportunities' (cited in Betts, 1978, p.77). Often, there simply is not time to think; a decision must be made and made quickly if, for example, life is to be preserved. In such cases, the 'principles of optimal analytic procedure are in many respects incompatible with the imperatives of the decision process' (Betts, 1978, p.63), but thinking and reflection should never be dismissed as antitheses of action, particularly when time is a lesser factor or when problems easily can be broken down into their component parts.

Policing and technology

Undoubtedly, the internet provides the police with many more opportunities to collect information than were available to them even in the very recent past. The question of how much information the police need to be effective and appropriately reflexive is an extremely interesting one. In that context, in the rush to discover new ways of fighting crime (in all its forms), traditional tools and techniques should not be disregarded. There is just as much of a need to improve the extrapolation of meaningful data from existing structured databases as there is for the development of big data analytics. Currently, big data's strength is in identifying who should be monitored, but without intruding into people's lives far more than citizens are yet willing to accept, it is unlikely that it will provide ground commanders with the 'when, where?' and so on often delivered by little data that conveys the requisite tactical advantage. In a society committed to a Peelian ideal, big data will not provide the silver bullet that policing seems always to be searching for any more than PP or social media. Each may help to deliver a more effective and reflexive police service in the future – that certainly is the police rhetoric – but there is little evidence that any one of them has yet influenced fundamental change in the organisation or the way in which it goes about its business. There may be no limits to what technology can offer in the information age. In some quarters, there certainly is a will to go much further in exploiting it to expose criminality, but there are profound questions to be answered about the necessity, the appropriateness and ultimately the legitimacy of such acts that go far beyond technical capacity or capability.

Looking ahead

For all their successes, the police need to make a much better case for their intelligence practices and they need to improve them in an era when the emphasis is so heavily on doing more with less. This penultimate section considers some of the ways that the credibility of intelligence practice might be enhanced and, perhaps even more importantly in terms of their long-term interests, how the police may develop their staff sufficiently that the work is worthy of the label 'profession'.

Regulatory certainty

The weight of expert opinion on the legislative framework for intelligence practice is that substantial change to both the legislative and oversight frameworks is essential. The development of legislation in this important area of policing has been characterised by fudge and drift. The current oversight regime, while superficially adequate, developed in an *ad hoc*, event-driven way. Solutions designed to address specific problems are not necessarily generalisable to other problems even when they share some of their characteristics. So, for example, some oversight commissioners are more generously resourced than others, which has meant that inspections cannot easily be standardised. Moreover, it was inevitable that a de facto committee of commissioners would differ in their interpretation of nebulous and context-specific concepts such as privacy and necessity and that only has added to the confusion of practitioners.

Proposals for a comprehensive overhaul of the current legislative and oversight regimes (by RUSI, 2015 and by Anderson, 2015) are currently on the table. Notwithstanding the detail of any future regulation, it has been argued that there should be 10 'enduring tests' for the state's invasion of individual privacy (RUSI, 2015, p.104). Notably, those include respect for the rule of law, justification for every intrusion and the consistent achievement of a balance between the degree of intrusion and the seriousness of the offence under investigation. In terms of operational practice, much of what has been proposed is little more than is required to conform to ECHR, but more radical proposals have been made for reform of the oversight regime. RUSI's recommendation is that a single independent organisation, the National Intelligence and Surveillance Office, take over the responsibilities of the seven existing commissioners and that power to authorise covert policing techniques in crime investigations is transferred from the executive to the judiciary.[5] On 4 November 2015, the Home Secretary published the Investigatory Powers Bill. In large part, the Bill is the government's response to calls from RUSI and others for urgent reform. Many, but by no means all, those concerns will be addressed in the new legislation.

The Home Office proposes a new Act that combines existing powers to obtain communications and data about communications. In the process, it promises to make the use of those powers more clear and understandable, but it also wants to extend them by implementing provisions for the retention of internet connection records; essentially, phone companies and internet service providers will be obliged to keep records of websites visited by every citizen for a period of 12 months. The police, SIAs and other public bodies will have the power to access those records. In terms of future oversight, it proposes a 'double-lock' for interception warrants. Secretaries of State will continue to play a role in the authorisation process, but warrants will not come into force until they have been approved by a judge. A new Investigatory Powers Commissioner will replace the existing system. These proposals may just be the opening salvo in a protracted engagement; much may change before the new Act is passed and it will be many months before we can be sure what the new arrangements will look like. Whatever the outcome, it is to be hoped that the new legislative and oversight regimes provide much greater clarity for practitioners than has existed hitherto.

An intelligence profession

There probably are as many definitions of 'profession' as there are of 'intelligence'. For the purposes of this analysis, a profession is a vocation, taken up by people who want to contribute to society, which requires skills acquired through practical experiences, specialised knowledge gained through prolonged academic training, and a commitment to ethical behaviour. Many intelligence analysts consider themselves professionals. Certainly, among intelligence staff, analysts usually are the best trained and best educated, but, as Chapter One demonstrated, it is questionable whether many of those in the policing milieu meet all of the essential criteria to achieve that distinction. The formalisation of practice through the APP, the introduction of a code of ethics and the ongoing work to establish national occupational standards for analysis and competencies for analysts via the IPP all represent progress towards the attainment of that status. The endeavour and entrepreneurship of those who have stimulated these initiatives is laudable, but there remains an obvious gap, which it is argued can be filled (and thus professional status achieved) only by scholarship, academic study and achievement at a high level.

There is a rich, layered and appropriately critical literature on intelligence practice in the context of national security. Much of that literature has been generated by individuals with a well-deserved reputation as senior statesmen in the intelligence milieu, having developed the craft of intelligence into a profession through long years of professional practice, scholarly endeavour and policy entrepreneurship. They merit the label 'intelligence visionaries'. With just a few exceptions (who are spared the embarrassment of being named here), they have few peers in the UK policing world. Nor is there much of a police intelligence literature to speak of.[6] There are many reasons for that. They include the dominance of the reactive policing paradigm over many years; the institution's obsession with omnicompetence (so that specialists seeking advancement rarely are permitted to remain in the same department – yes, on promotion the subject expert on prison intelligence really was appointed as the force lead for roads policing); and, not least, the anti-intellectualism of policing.

In consequence, policing largely lacks an institutional memory worthy of the name and practitioners are unable to draw on the kinds of sage advice (in the form of reflective commentaries on intelligence practice, records of near-real time evaluations of significant events and scholar/practitioner evaluations of intelligence successes and failures) that, over time, can enrich their own practice and help them to develop the brands of insight and authority in the field that usually are associated with the professions. Intelligence staff also need a broader set of skills, abilities and experiences that can only come from exposure to different dimensions of intelligence work, better networking and greater professional knowledge.

New technologies promise to streamline the analytical process, but it is difficult to see a future in which the analyst's professional skills of insight, judgement and advocacy will not be required. Historically, civilian analysts, and later researchers, were 'parachuted into' existing intelligence structures. Some research respondents said that their roles had been (or were about to be) changed fundamentally by technology. Those committed to the advancement of police intelligence practice will see this as an opportunity to help staff add to their practical abilities the critical thinking and writing skills that scholars and researchers such as Heuer (1999) have been arguing for many years are essential to the work. However, the public services are operating in an age of austerity and, in consequence, many forces are taking the other option, to rely more heavily on technology and dispense with the services of what they have determined are 'back-office' staff. The debate over the true status of intelligence staff as support or frontline resources is an old one. A case can be made for either. Given the pressure on forces to finds cost savings, it is understandable why many would favour the former; the axe has to fall somewhere, but the discourse is skewed by the tendency to post officers who have de facto been retired from active service through sickness or injury to intelligence units and the failure (identified by many researchers) to recognise the value of intelligence.

Some elements of the institution see value in developing a more mature, more reflexive discourse within the organisation and in building new relationships with individuals and institutions outside of the UK policing bubble with the aim of furthering the professional development of staff. As this analysis has shown, there may be much that the military, SIAs and police can learn from each other about intelligence practice if there is the will to develop that relationship. The engagement with academia both in the UK and in the US is to be applauded, but if practitioners are to get the recognition as professionals they feel they deserve, policing will need to understand that this is a long-term commitment to reconfiguring the intelligence workforce in developmental and incremental ways that will test the patience and resolve of managers conditioned to short-termism.

Early results are important in encouraging support and participation and to gain credibility for the efforts being made. The recent appointment of NIM 'champions' in each of the 43 forces, with the responsibility *inter alia* to communicate key messages about intelligence to the front line, should be seen in that light, but the momentum must be sustained. Policing has made a promising start in overhauling the NIM, but the pace of change in the intelligence milieu (in the context both of technology and of law) means that standing pat is not an option. Policing must press ahead with plans to professionalise the intelligence workforce, advance wider knowledge of intelligence and its benefits, and integrate partners more fully into the work.

The last word

It is axiomatic that the outcomes of organisational reform always are limited by the extent to which decision makers believe that change is both in their best interests and will deliver practical benefits.[7] It is not an over-dramatisation to say that police intelligence practice is at a crossroads and that reform is needed; the kinds of inadequacies identified in this book undermine policing's efforts to meet the threats and challenges of modernity. It is to be hoped that police commanders and their political overseers will recognise the benefits of that change. The effectiveness and efficacy of intelligence practice are dependent on three discrete but complementary elements: the legislative framework; oversight arrangements; and professional praxis. The justified clamour for meaningful change in the first two has reached a crescendo with the publication of the Anderson and RUSI reports in 2015; substantial modifications to both are inevitable. Historically, the policing institution has been a significant actor in structuring and shaping political behaviour. Although its influence on government now is much diminished, as it looks inward following the reform of its own executive, practitioners must hope that it quickly will find both its voice and a way for that voice to be heard in the debate.

The institution must look to itself to reshape praxis. Shortcomings in the intelligence workforce and in the management of intelligence are well understood; there is a direct correlation between the two. If the key determinant of intelligence success really is the ethical collection and analysis of information precise enough to deliver effective operational responses, policing needs experts in those endeavours. That means redefining staffs' roles, finding ways to share knowledge held by specialists (both within and without the institution) with practitioners, making a far greater commitment to the professional development of the workforce and more obviously valuing its contribution to policing and the communities it serves. None of these things removes the element of uncertainty from the work. Only rarely is the complete picture known. Intelligence failure will continue to be inevitable, but if policing wants to convince its stakeholders and the public that the work is being carried on diligently and professionally and that the institution can be trusted with the necessary evil that is intelligence practice, it cannot continue to rely on an analogue system in a digital age.

Notes

1 *A priori*, a recent NCA recruitment campaign for experienced investigators and intelligence officers may well be linked to these events.

2 In the past, that was one of the roles performed by Special Branch, but the exposure of its inadequacies by the London 7/7 and 21/7 bombings led to the establishment of CTC and the PCTN. There was, therefore, an obvious need for a new method of processing data originating from the SIAs, which the CIUs have provided.

3 Edward Snowden is a former US National Security Agency subcontractor who leaked top secret information about the surveillance activities of the NSA and its partners. To many he is a hero but to the US state, which has charged him with espionage offences, he is a traitor and criminal. Currently, he lives in exile in Russia where he has been granted asylum.

4 The London riots of 2011 suggest that there may be exceptions to that rule.

5 In cases involving national security, the suggestion is that the activity will continue to be authorised by the Secretary of State subject to review by a judicial commissioner.

6 Reference here is exclusively to the study of the discipline of intelligence. There is a much wider literature on ILP, which is a valuable resource for scholars and practitioners.

7 The failure of NIM is testament to that.

Further reading

College of Policing (2015): *Code of Ethics* at https://www.app.college.police.uk/code-of-ethics/?s=code+of+ethics

Davies, P; Gustafson, K; Rigden, I (2013), The Intelligence Cycle is dead, long live the Intelligence Cycle in M. Phythian (Ed.), *Understanding the Intelligence Cycle*. Abingdon: Routledge pp.56-75.

Gentry, JA (2010), Assessing Intelligence Performance in LK. Johnson (Ed.), *Oxford Handbook of National Security Intelligence*. New York, NY: OUP, pp.87-103.

Gill, P and Phythian, M (2012), *Intelligence in an Insecure World* (2nd Ed.) London: Polity.

Hulnick, A (2013), Seeking better models in M. Phythian (Ed.) *Understanding the Intelligence Cycle*. Abingdon: Routledge, pp.149-60

ISC (2015). *Women in the UK Intelligence Community*. London: HMSO

Kleinig, J (1996), *Ethics of Policing*. New York, NY: CUP.

Epilogue

I recall one very long day at the office (more accurately, two nights and one day), when I was new in post at a police intelligence unit, directing operational teams. The shift drew to its close with me, desperate for sleep, still trying to make sense of events that included the long-analysed and plotted armed interdiction of two multi-kilo shipments of Class A drugs in different parts of the country; three unanticipated armed deployments to preserve the life of one of the conspirators (who, it emerged, was wrongly suspected by the group of being an informer); numerous furtive telephone conversations with colleagues and with the CPS on how best to deal with a double-crossing CHIS (ironically, not the individual suspected by the traffickers); and, not least, the crashing of two surveillance cars resulting in the occupants receiving injuries sufficient to put them and their vehicles out of action for the day.

My line manager's response to my incredulity at the sheer complexity of the events that had taken place in such a short period confirmed him as the master of understatement I had always known him to be, but also gave me the kind of insight into the work that, in the following weeks, months and years I would find invaluable. Having listened to me in silence, his only comment as he left the room to address the challenges of his similarly frenetic day was, 'What do you expect Adrian? The work is lively.' I have reflected often on his sagacity and on the way that for me that one word 'lively' captures so many facets of intelligence practice at the sharp end. Lively – yes, it certainly can be that.

References

Audit Commission (1993) *Helping with Enquiries: Tackling Crime Effectively*. London: Audit Commission

ACPO/NPIA (National Police Improvement Agency) (2008) *Practice Advice on Analysis*. London: NPIA

Akers, RL (1990) 'Rational choice, deterrence, and social learning theory in criminology: the path not taken', *Journal of Criminal Law and Criminology*, vol 81, no. 5, pp.653–76

Alison, L; Power, N; van den Heuvel, C; Humann, M; Palasinksi, M; Crego, J (2015) 'Decision inertia: deciding between least worst outcomes in emergency responses to disasters', *Journal of Occupational and Organizational Psychology*, vol 88, no. 2, pp.295–321

Anderson, D (2015) *A Question of Trust – Report of the Investigatory Powers Review*. London: Anderson

Anon (nd) 'Phillip B. Davidson, Jr. and army intelligence doctrine', http://huachuca.army.mil/files/History_MDAVID.PDF

Armstrong, J (2015) 'Durham Chief Constable Mike Barton says police national database is helping in organised crime fight', *Chronicle Live*, 27 February, www.chroniclelive.co.uk/news/north-east-news/durham-chief-constable-mike-barton-8725163

Bacon, F (1605) *The advancement of learning*, London: Henrie Tomes

Ball, K and Wood, DM (eds) *A Report on the Surveillance Society for the Information Commissioner*. London: Surveillance Studies Network

Ballaschk, J (2015) 'In the unseen realm: transnational intelligence sharing in the European Union – Challenges to fundamental rights and democratic legitimacy', *Stanford Journal of International Law*, vol 51, no. 1, pp.19–51.

Baumber, G (1975) *Report of ACPO Sub-Committee on Intelligence*. London: ACPO

BBC (2014) 'UK terror threat: "up to five" plots stopped in 2014', 23 November, www.bbc.co.uk/news/uk-30166946

Beck, U (2009) 'Critical theory of world risk society: a cosmopolitan vision', *Constellations*, vol. 16, no. 1, pp.3–22

Beckford, M (2015) 'National Chaos Agency: seven crime chiefs quit "Britain's FBI" as morale plummets less than two years after force was set up', *Daily Mail*, 19 July, www.dailymail.co.uk/news/article-3166769

Betts, RK (1978) 'Analysis, war, and decision: why intelligence failures are inevitable', *World Politics*, vol. 31, no. 1, pp.61–89

Bhatt, H (2006) 'RIPA 2000: a human rights examination', *International Journal of Human Rights*, vol. 10, no. 3, pp.285-314

Bichard, M (2004) *The Bichard Inquiry Report*. London: HMSO

Billingsley, R (2009) *Covert Human Intelligence Sources: The 'Unlovely' Face of Police Work*. Hook: Waterside Press

Birkett, N (1957) *Report of the Committee of Privy Councillors Appointed to Inquire into the Interception of Communication*. London: HMSO

boyd, D and Crawford, K (2012) 'Critical questions for big data', *Information, Communication & Society*, vol. 15, no. 5, pp. 662-79.

Brandon, M; Sidebotham, P; Bailey, S; Belderson, P (2011) *A Study of Recommendations Arising from Serious Case Reviews 2009-10*. London: DfE

Bristow, K (2015) 'Transnational organised crime as a national security threat', Speech given at George Washington University on 29 January 2015, www.nationalcrimeagency.gov.uk/publications/503-dg-washington-speech-jan-2015/file

Brodeur, J-P (1983) 'High and low policing: remarks about the policing of political activities', *Social Problems*, vol. 30, no. 5, pp.507-21

Brodeur, J-P (2010) *The policing web*, New York, NY: OUP

Buneman, P; Khanna, S; Chiew- Tan, W (2001) 'Why and where: a characterization of data provenance', in J Van den Bussche and V Vianu (eds) *International Conference on Database Theory*. New York, NY: Springer, pp.316-30

Bures, O (2008) 'Europol's fledgling counterterrorism role', *Terrorism and Political Violence*, vol. 20, no. 4, pp.498-517.

Butler, Lord (2004) *Review of Intelligence on Weapons of Mass Destruction: Report of a Committee of Privy Counsellors*. London: HMSO

Cabinet Office (2013) *Government Security Classifications*. London: Cabinet Office

Chainey, S and Ratcliffe, J (2005) *GIS and Crime Mapping*. London: Wiley

Cheshire Constabulary (nd) 'About us', www.cheshire.police.uk/about-us/departments-and-structure/specialist-units/intelligence.aspx

Clark, R (2000) 'Informers and corruption', in R Billingsley, T Nemitz and P Bean (eds) *Informers: Policing, Policy, Practice*. Cullompton: Willan, pp.38-49

Clausewitz, Von C (1874) 'On war', translated by Colonel J.J. Graham, www.gutenberg.org/files/1946/1946-h/1946-h.htm

Clutterbuck, L (2002) 'An accident of history? The evolution of counter terrorism methodology in the Metropolitan Police from 1829 to 1901, with particular reference to the influence of extreme Irish Nationalist activity', Unpublished PhD thesis, University of Portsmouth

CoP (College of Policing) (2013a) 'Collection and recording', www.app.college.police.uk/app-content/information-management/management-of-police-information/collection-and-recording

CoP (2013b) 'Evaluation', www.app.college.police.uk/app-content/information-management/management-of-police-information/evaluation

CoP (2013c) 'Risk', www.app.college.police.uk/app-content/risk-2/risk

CoP (2014a) 'Research and analysis', www.app.college.police.uk/app-content/intelligence-management/analysis

CoP (2014b) *Police Code of Ethics*. London: CoP

CoP (2014c) 'National Decision Model', www.app.college.police.uk/app-content/national-decision-model/the-national-decision-model

CoP (2015a) *Intelligence Management*. London: CoP

CoP (2015b) *Human Rights and Policing*. London: CoP

CoP (2015c) 'Schengen Information System (second generation) SIS II', www.app.college.police.uk/app-content/investigations/european-investigations/schengen-information-system

CoP (2015d) 'Intelligence report', www.app.college.police.uk/app-content/intelligence-management/intelligence-report

Cope, N (2004) 'Crime analysis: principles and practice', in T Newburn (ed) *Handbook of Policing*. Cullompton: Willan, pp.340-62

Cox, B; Shirley, J; Short, M (1977) *The Fall of Scotland Yard*. Norwich: Fletcher and Sons

CPS (Crown Prosecution Service) (2015a) 'Attorney General's guidelines on disclosure', www.cps.gov.uk/legal/a_to_c/attorney_generals_guidelines_on_disclosure

CPS (2015b) 'Chapter 27: Dealing with intercept product', www.cps.gov.uk/legal/d_to_g/disclosure_manual/disclosure_manual_chapter_27

Creedon, M (2014) *Operation Herne Report 2*. Ashbourne: Derbyshire Constabulary

Crum, R (2014) 'Twitter's 23 million "bot" question mark', *Market Watch*, http://blogs.marketwatch.com/thetell/2014/08/12

CSC (Chief Surveillance Commissioner) (2015) 'Annual report of the Chief Surveillance Commissioner for 2013 to 2014', www.gov.uk/government/publications/annual-report-of-the-chief-surveillance-commissioner-for-2013-to-2014

CSPL (Committee for Standards in Public Life) (1995) *Seven Principles of Public Life*. London: HMSO

Dahl, EJ (2013) *Intelligence and Surprise Attack: Failure and Success from Pearl Harbor to 9/11 and Beyond*. Washington, DC: Georgetown University Press

Dane, E; Rockmann, KW; Pratt, MG (2012) 'When should I trust my gut? Linking domain expertise to intuitive decision-making effectiveness', *Organizational Behavior and Human Decision Processes*, vol 119, no. 2, pp.187–194

Davies, P; Gustafson, K; Rigden, I (2013) 'The intelligence cycle is dead, long live the intelligence cycle', in M Phythian (ed) *Understanding the Intelligence Cycle*. Abingdon: Routledge, pp.56-75

Davis, EF III; Alves, AA; Sklansky, DA (2014) *Social Media and Police Leadership: Lessons from Boston. New Perspectives in Policing Bulletin*. Washington, DC: U.S. Department of Justice, National Institute of Justice

Davis, J (2002) 'Sherman Kent and the profession of intelligence analysis', *Sherman Kent Center Occasional Papers*, vol. 1, no. 5, www.cia.gov/library/kent-center-occasional-papers/vol1no5.htm

Dennis, M (2014) 'Figuring out the questions to be answered simplifies the search for information within unstructured data', *IBM Systems Magazine*, www.ibmsystemsmag.com/mainframe/trends/Modernization/unstructured_data

Den Boer, M (2015) 'Counter-terrorism, security and intelligence in the EU: governance challenges for collection, exchange and analysis', *Intelligence and National Security*, vol. 30, no. 2-3, pp.402-19

DiMaggio, PJ and Powell, WW (1983) 'The iron cage revisited – institutional isomorphism and collective rationality in organizational fields', *American Sociological Review*, vol 48, no. 2 pp.147-60

DPP (Director of Public Prosecutions) (2014) 'Guidelines on prosecuting cases involving communications sent via social media', www.cps.gov.uk/legal/a_to_c/communications_sent_via_social_media/index.html

Duggan, W (2004) *Napoleon's Glance: The Secrets of Strategy*. New York, NY: Nation Books

Durkheim, E and Allcock, J (eds) (1983) *Pragmatism and Sociology*. Cambridge: CUP, www.marxists.org/reference/subject/philosophy/works/fr/durkheim.htm

Elliott, T (2013) '7 definitions of big data you should know about', http://timoelliott.com/blog/2013/07/7-definitions-of-big-data-you-should-know-about.html

EU (European Union) (2009) 'Acts adopted under Title VI of the Eu Treaty' *Official Journal of the European Union*, www.europol.europa.eu/sites/default/files/council_decision.pdf

eu-LISA (2014) 'Annual activity report', www.eulisa.europa.eu/Publications/Corporate/eu-LISA%20Annual%20%20Activity%20Report%202014.pdf

Europol (2015) 'About us', www.europol.europa.eu/content/page/about-us

FBI (Federal Bureau of Investigation) (2015) 'The intelligence cycle', www.fbi.gov/about-us/intelligence/intelligence-cycle

Feldman, B (2012) 'Behavioral profile of an effective German leader of a global health company', Master's dissertation, University of Twente, http://essay.utwente.nl/61950/1/MasterThesis_BarbaraFeldmann.pdf

Fenwick, H (2000) *Civil Rights: New Labour, Freedom and the Human Rights Act*.
Harlow: Longman

Fogarty, K (2012) 'Big data plus police work: good partners?', *Information Week*, 24 July, www.informationweek.com/software/information-management/big-data-plus-police-work-good-partners/d/d-id/1105482?

Fuller, G (1991) 'Intelligence, immaculately conceived', *The National Interest*, vol 26 pp. 95–99

Gani, A (2014) What is the European convention on human rights? *The Guardian* 3 October http://www.theguardian.com/law/2014/oct/03/what-is-european-convention-on-human-rights-echr

Gentry, JA (2010) 'Assessing intelligence performance', in LK Johnson (ed)
Oxford Handbook of National Security Intelligence. New York, NY: OUP, pp.87–103

Gill, P (2000) *Rounding up the Usual Suspects*. Aldershot: Ashgate

Gill, P (2009) 'The Intelligence and Security Committee and the challenge of security networks', *Review of International Studies*, vol 35, no. 4, pp.929–41

Gill, P and Phythian, M (2012) *Intelligence in an Insecure World* (2nd edn). London: Polity

Gilmore, M (2013) 'Chief tells police to end risk-averse culture in new shake-up', *Yorkshire Post*, 9 November, www.yorkshirepost. co.uk/news/main-topics/general-news/chief-tells-police-to-end-risk-averse-culture-in-new-shake-up-1-6230682

Gottschalk, P (2010) 'Theories of financial crime', *Journal of Financial Crime*, vol. 17, no. 2, pp.210-22

Greathouse, J (2012) 'Celebrities with the most (allegedly) fake Twitter followers', 27 August, www.forbes.com/sites/ johngreathouse/2012/08/27

Grieve, J (2004) 'Lawfully audacious: a reflective journey', in C Harfield, J Grieve and A MacVean (eds) *Handbook of Intelligent Policing: Consilience, Crime Control, and Community Safety*. Oxford: OUP, pp.13-24

Gries, D (nd) 'Openness and secrecy', www.cia.gov/library/center-for-the-study-of-intelligence/kent-csi/vol37no1/pdf/v37i1a01p.pdf

Hall, M (2013) 'Former head of MI6 threatens to expose secrets of Iraq "dodgy dossier"', *The Telegraph*, 21 July, www.telegraph.co.uk/news/ uknews/10193204/Former-head-of-MI6-threatens-to-expose-secrets-of-Iraq-dodgy-dossier.html

Hammond, KR (2000) *Judgments under stress*. New York, NY: OUP

Harfield, C (2009) *Blackstone's Police Operational Handbook: Practice and Procedure*. Oxford: OUP

Harfield, C and Harfield, K (2008) *Intelligence, Investigation, Community and Partnership*. Oxford: OUP

Harfield, C and Harfield, K (2012) *Covert Investigation* (3rd edn). Oxford: OUP

Harford, M (2011) 'In praise of pragmatism', www.independent.co.uk/ news/world/politics/in-praise-of-pragmatism-2293820.html

Harford, T (2014) 'Big data: are we making a big mistake?', http:// timharford.com/2014/04

Harper, WR and Harris, DH (1975) 'The application of link analysis to police intelligence', *Human Factors*, vol 17, no. 2, pp.157-164

Harris, DH (1978) 'Development of a computer-based program for criminal intelligence analysis', *Human Factors*, vol. 20, no. 1, pp.47-56

Hayes, B (2006) *The Future of Europol: More Powers, Less Regulation, Precious Little Debate*. London: Statewatch

Heaton, R (2010) 'We could be criticized! Policing and risk aversion', *Policing*, vol. 5, no. 1, pp.75-86

Herman, M (2001) *Intelligence Services in the Information Age: Theory and Practice*. New York, NY: Frank Cass

Heuer, R (1999) *The Psychology of Intelligence Analysis*. Washington, DC: Central Intelligence Agency

Hirsch, C (2002) 'Policing undercover agents in the United Kingdom: whether the Regulation of Investigatory Powers Act complies with regional human rights obligations', *Fordham International Law Journal*, vol. 25, no. 5, pp. 1282-334

HCHASC (House of Commons Home Affairs Select Committee) (2009) 'The work of the Serious Organised Crime Agency', www.publications.parliament.uk/pa/cm200809/cmselect/cmhaff/730/73004.htm

HLEUC (House Of Lords European Union Committee) (2008) *EUROPOL: Coordinating the Fight Against Serious and Organised Crime*, 29th Report of Session 2007-08. London: HMSO

HLSCC (House of Lords Select Committee on the Constitution) (2009) *Surveillance: Citizens and the State*, HL Paper 18-I, www.publications.parliament.uk/pa/ld200809/ldselect/ldconst/18/18.pdf

HMIC (Her Majesty's Inspectorate of Constabulary) (2014a) *Inspection of Undercover Policing in England and Wales*. London: HMIC

HMIC (2014b) *Policing in Austerity: Rising to the Challenge*. London: HMIC

HMIC (2015) *Building the Picture: An Inspection of Police Information Management*. London: HMIC

Hogan-Howe, B (2011) 'Howe to get ahead', *Police Review*, vol. 119, no. 6152, pp.14-15

Home Office (1984) *Guidelines on the Use of Technical Equipment in Police Surveillance Operations*. Unpublished administrative guidelines for police forces

Home Office (2010) *The National Security Strategy: A Strong Britain in an Age of Uncertainty*. London: Home Office

Home Office (2011a) *Local to Global: Reducing the Risk from Organised Crime*. London: HMSO

Home Office (2011b) *CONTEST: The United Kingdom's Strategy for Countering Terrorism (version 3)*. London: Home Office

Home Office (2013) *Serious and Organised Crime Strategy*. London: Home Office

Home Office (2014a) *RIPA Codes*. London: Home Office

Home Office (2014b) *The Serious and Organised Crime Strategy: Annual Report for 2014*. London: Home Office

Hughes, D and Bell, H (1995) *Moltke on the Art of War: Selected Writings*. New York, NY: Presidio Press

Hulnick, A (2013) 'Seeking better models', in M Phythian (ed) *Understanding the Intelligence Cycle*. Abingdon: Routledge, pp.149-60

Hunt, P; Saunders, J; Hollywood, JS (2014) *Evaluation of the Shreveport Predictive Policing Experiment*. Santa Monica, CA: Rand Corporation

IBM (2013) 'The four Vs of big data', www.ibmbigdatahub.com/infographic/four-vs-big-data

Innes, M; Fielding, N; Cope, N (2005) 'The appliance of science? The theory and practice of crime intelligence analysis', *British Journal of Criminology*, vol 45, no. 1, pp.39-57

Internet Live Stats (2015) Real Time Statistics Project website, www.internetlivestats.com/statistics

Interpol (2013) 'Interpol annual report 2013', www.interpol.int/News-and-media/Publications#n627

Interpol (2015) 'Criminal intelligence analysis', www.interpol.int/INTERPOL-expertise/Criminal-Intelligence-analysis

IOCC (Report of the Interception of Communications Commissioner) (2015) *Report of the Interception of Communications Commissioner: March 2015*. London: IOCC

ISC (Intelligence and Security Committee of Parliament) (2006) *Report into the London Terrorist Attacks on 7 July 2005*. London: HMSO

ISC (2009) *Could 7/7 Have Been Prevented? Review of the Intelligence on the London Terrorist Attacks on 7 July 2005*. London: HMSO

ISC (2014a) *Intelligence and Security Committee of Parliament, Annual Report 2013-2014*. London: HMSO

ISC (2014b) *Report on the Intelligence Relating to the Murder of Fusilier Lee Rigby*. London: HMSO

ISC (2015) *Women in the UK Intelligence Community*. London: HMSO

James, A (2013) *Examining Intelligence-led Policing*. Basingstoke: Palgrave MacMillan

James, W (1904) 'What is pragmatism?', www.marxists.org/reference/subject/philosophy/works/us/james.htm

Jervis, R (2011) 'Why intelligence and policymakers clash', *Political Science Quarterly*, vol. 125, no. 2, pp. 185-204

Joh, EE (2014) 'Policing by Numbers: Big Data and the Fourth Amendment', *Washington Law Review*, vol 89, no 1, pp.185-204

Kafka, F (1946) *The Great Wall of China: Stories and reflections*, New York, NY: Schocken Books

Kahler, S (2012) 'Big data: what's the big deal?', Paper presented at Kansas City Big Data Event, 12 September, www.kcitp.com/2012/09/03/big-data-kansas-city-technology-events

Kahneman, D (2011) *Thinking Fast and Slow*. New York, NY: Penguin

Kaplan, AM and Haenlein, M (2010) 'Users of the world, unite! The challenges and opportunities of social media', *Business Horizons*, vol. 53, no. 1, pp.59-68

Keim, D; Mansmann, F; Schneidewind, J; Thomas, J: Hartmut Z (2008) 'Visual analytics: scope and challenges', in SJ Simoff et al (eds) *Visual Data Mining*. Springer-Verlag: Berlin, pp.76-90

Kemshall, H (2001) *Risk Assessment and Management of Known Sexual and Violent Offenders: A Review of Current Issues*. Home Office Police Research Series Paper 140, London: Home Office

Kirk, CJ (2013) 'The demise of decision-making: how information superiority degrades our ability to make decisions', Paper submitted to the US Naval War College faculty in partial satisfaction of the requirements of the Joint Military Operations Department

Klein, G (2008) 'Naturalistic decision making', *Human Factors*, vol. 50, no. 3, pp.456-60

Kleinig, J (1996) *The Ethics of Policing*. New York, NY: CUP

Kleiven, M (2005) 'Where's the intelligence in the National Intelligence Model?', Unpublished MSc dissertation, Institute of Criminal Justice Studies, University of Portsmouth

Klerks, P (2001) 'The network paradigm applied to criminal organisations: theoretical nit-picking or a relevant doctrine for investigators? Recent developments in the Netherlands', *Connections*, vol. 24, no. 3, pp.53-65

Klockars, CB (1980) 'The Dirty Harry problem', *Annals of the American Academy of Political and Social Science*, vol. 452, Police and Violence, pp.33-47

LABPC (London Assembly Budget and Performance Committee) (2013) *Smart Policing: How the Metropolitan Police Service Can Make Better Use of Technology*, Report of the London Assembly's Budget and Performance Committee, London: London Assembly

Lewis, P; Newburn, T; Ball, J; Procter, R; Vis, F; Voss, A (2011) *Reading the Riots: Investigating England's Summer of Disorder*, London: *The Guardian*/LSE

Lipshitz, R (1993) 'Converging themes in the study of decision making in realistic settings', in GA Klein, J Orasanu, R Calderwood and CE Zsambok (eds) *Decision Making in Action: Models and Methods*. Norwood, NJ: Ablex, pp.103-37

Lloyd, IJ (1986), The Interception of Communications Act, 1985. *The Modern Law Review* Volume 49, Issue 1, pp.86-95

Lobban, I (2014) 'Valedictory speech', www.gchq.gov.uk/press_and_media/speeches/Pages/Iain-Lobban-valedictory-speech-as-delivered.aspx

MacVean, A (2008) 'The governance of intelligence', in C. Harfield, J. Grieve and A. MacVean (eds) *Handbook of Intelligent Policing: Consilience, Crime Control, and Community Safety*. Oxford: OUP, pp.63-74

MacVean, A and Harfield, C (2008) 'Science or sophistry: issues in managing analysts and their products', in C Harfield, A MacVean, J Grieve and D Phillips (eds). *Handbook of Intelligent Policing: Consilience, Crime Control, and Community Safety*. Oxford: OUP, pp.93-104

Mainas, E (2012) 'The analysis of criminal and terrorist organisations as social network structures: a quasi-experimental study', *International Journal of Police Science and Management*, vol. 14, no. 3, pp.264-82

Marx, GT (1988) *Undercover: Police Surveillance in America*. Berkeley, CA: University of California Press

McKay, S (2011) *Covert Policing Law and Practice*. London: OUP

McKay, S (2015) *Covert Policing Law and Practice* (2nd edn). London: OUP

McDowell, D (2009) *Strategic Intelligence: A Handbook for Practitioners, Managers, and Users* (revised edn). Toronto: Scarecrow Press

MoD (Ministry of Defence) (2011) *Understanding and Intelligence Support to Joint Operations* (3rd edn). Shrivenham: MoD Development, Concepts and Doctrine Centre

Moe, TM (1979) 'On the scientific status of rational models', *American Political Science Review*, vol. 23, pp.215-43

Moseley, A; Cotterill S; Richardson, L (2012) 'Can nudging create the Big Society? Experiments in civic behaviour and implications for the voluntary and public sectors', *Voluntary Sector Review*, vol. 3, no. 2, pp.265-74

Motti, J (2014) 'Twitter acknowledges 23 million active users are actually bots', *Tech Times*, 12 August, www.techtimes.com/articles/12840/20140812/twitter-acknowledges-14-percent-users-bots-5-percent-spam-bots.htm

Moysey, S (2008) *The Road to Balcombe Street: The IRA Reign of Terror in London*. Binghamton, NY: Haworth Press

MPS (Metropolitan Police Service) (2014) *ONE MET Total Technology 2014-17*. London: MPS

NCA (nd) 'Learn more about the NCA: leading the UK's fight to cut serious and organised crime', www.nationalcrimeagency.gov.uk/publications/50-nca-awareness-leaflet/file

NCA (National Crime Agency) (2014) *UK National Strategic Assessment of Serious and Organised Crime 2014*. London: NCA

NCARRB (National Crime Agency Rewards and Recognition Board) (2014) *National Crime Agency Remuneration Review Body, First Report 2014.* London: NCA

NPIA (National Police Improvement Agency) (2011) 'The NIM', www.npia.police.uk/en/9015.htm

Occhipinti, J (2015) 'Still moving toward a European FBI? Re-examining the politics of EU police cooperation', *Intelligence and National Security*, vol. 30, no. 2-3, pp.234-58

Omand, D (2010) 'Transcript of evidence to the Chilcot Inquiry', www.iraqinquiry.org.uk/media/44187/20100120pm-omand-final.pdf

Omand, D; Bartlett, D; Miller, C (2012) 'Introducing social media intelligence (SOCMINT)', *Intelligence and National Security*, vol. 27, no. 6, pp. 801-23

O'Neill, O (2002) *A Question of Trust: The BBC Reith Lectures 2002.* Cambridge: CUP

Osborn, N (2012) 'To what degree have the non-police public services adopted the National Intelligence Model? What benefits could the National Intelligence Model deliver?', Unpublished Professional Doctorate thesis, University of Portsmouth

Palmer, A (2009) 'Only incompetence will save us from Orwell's surveillance state', *Daily Telegraph*, 7 March, www.telegraph.co.uk/comment/4953396/Only-incompetence-will-save-us-from-Orwells-surveillance-state.html

Pearce, R (1978) *Report of the ACPO Working Party on a Structure of Criminal Intelligence Offices.* London: ACPO

Perry, WL; McInnis, B; Price, CC; Smith, SS; Hollywood, J (2013) *Predictive Policing: The Role of Crime Forecasting in Law Enforcement Operations.* Santa Monica, CA: RAND Corporation

Peterson, M (2003) 'The challenge for the political analyst', *Studies in Intelligence*, vol. 47, no. 1, pp.51-6

Pillar, C (2009) 'Valuing knowledge: a deontological approach', *Ethic Theory Moral Practice*, vol 12, issue 4, pp. 413-28

Police Foundation (2014) *Police Use of Social Media.* London: Police Foundation

POST (Parliamentary Office of Science and Technology) (2014) *Big Data, Crime and Security*, Report of the Houses of Parliament, Parliamentary Office of Science and Technology. London: HMSO

PredPol (2015) 'About PredPol', www.predpol.com/about

PSA (Police Superintendents' Association) (2013) 'National Crime Agency – your questions answered', www.policesupers.com/national-crime-agency-your-questions-answered

Punch, M (2013) *Police Corruption: Exploring Police Deviance and Crime.* Abingdon: Routledge

Phythian, M (2013) (ed) *Understanding the intelligence cycle,* London: Routledge

Ratcliffe, A (1986) *Report of the ACPO Working Party on Operational Intelligence.* London: ACPO

Ratcliffe, J (2008) *Intelligence-Led Policing.* Cullompton: Willan

Reiner, R (2007) *Law and Order: An Honest Citizen's Guide to Crime and Control.* Cambridge: Polity Press

Reuss-Ianni (1982) *Street cops and management cops,* Herndon, VA: Transaction Publishers

Richards, J (2010) *The Art and Science of Intelligence Analysis.* London: OUP

Robinson, G (2003) 'Risk assessment', in W-H Chui and M Nellis (eds) *Moving Probation Forward: Evidence, Arguments and Practice.* Harlow: Pearson, pp. 227–41

Rollington, A (2013) *Strategic Intelligence for the 21st Century: The Mosaic Method.* Oxford: OUP

Rose McGrory (2015) 'UK Social Media Statistics for 2015', www.rosemcgrory.co.uk/2015/01/06/uk-social-media-statistics-for-2015

Rosello, VM (1991) 'Clausewitz's contempt for intelligence', *Parameters, Journal of the Security Studies Institute,* Spring, pp.103–14

Rowley, M (2013) *MPS Response to London Assembly Budget & Performance Committee Report: Smart Policing.* London: MPS

RUSI (Royal United Services Institute) (2015) *A Democratic Licence to Operate Report of the Independent Surveillance Review.* London: RUSI

Safjański, T (2013) 'Barriers to the operational effectiveness of Europol', *Internal Security,* vol. 5, no. 1, pp.53–69

Schraagen, JM; Militello, L; Ormerod, T; Lipshitz, R (eds) (2008) *Naturalistic Decision Making and Macrocognition.* Burlington, VT: Ashgate

Scott, J (2000) *Social Network Analysis: A Handbook.* London: Sage Publications

Shakespeare, W (2001) (original work 1603) *The Tragedy of Hamlet Prince of Denmark.* New York, NY: Bartleby Press

Sheptycki, J (2004) 'Organizational pathologies in police intelligence systems: some contributions to the lexicon of intelligence-led policing', *European Journal of Criminology,* vol, 1, no. 3, pp.307–32

Shvarts, A (2001) 'The Russian mafia: do rational choice models apply?', *Michigan Sociological Review,* vol. 15 (Fall), pp.29–63

Simon, P (2013) *The Business Case for Big Data.* Hoboken, NJ: Wiley

Skocpol, T (1992) *Protecting Soldiers and Mothers: The Political Origins of Social Policy in the United States.* Cambridge, MA: Belknap Press

SOCA (Serious Organised Crime Agency) (2010) *Serious Organised Crime Agency Annual Report and Accounts 2009 to 2010.* London: SOCA

Sommers, J (2013) 'The interview: Europol DG Rob Wainwright', www.policeoracle.com/news/Terrorism+and+Allied+Matte rs/2013/Oct/31/The-Interview-Europol-Director-General-Rob-Wainwright_73247.html

Spencer, JR (2009) 'Telephone tap evidence and administrative detention in the United Kingdom', in M Wade and A Maljevic (eds) *A War on Terror? The European Stance on a New Threat, Changing Laws and Human Rights Implications.* New York, NY: Springer, pp.373-400

Sproat, P (2011) 'The Serious Organised Crime Agency and the National Crime Squad: a comparison of their output from open source materials', *Policing & Society*, vol. 21, no. 3, pp. 343-51

Stanier, I (2013) 'Contemporary organisational pathologies in police information sharing: new contributions to Sheptycki's lexicon of intelligence led policing', Unpublished Professional Doctorate thesis, London Metropolitan University

Stelfox, P (2009) *Criminal Investigation: An Introduction to Principles and Practice.* London: Routledge

Stevens, J (2001) 'Intelligence-led policing, Paper presented at 2nd World Conference on Modern Criminal Investigation, Organized Crime and Human Rights, Durban, South Africa

Strang, S (2000) *Project SLEIPNIR: An Analytical Technique for Operational Priority Setting.* Ontario: RCMP

Syal, R (2014) 'Judge criticises National Crime Agency over collapse of fraud trial', 2 December, *The Guardian*, www.theguardian.com/ law/2014/dec/02/judge-criticises-national-crime-agency-fraud-trial

Taylor, H (2012) *Social Media for Social Change: Using the Internet to Tackle Intolerance.* London: Institute for Strategic Dialogue

Taylor, J (2013) '7% of Twitter users are not human', *Our Social Times*, http://oursocialtimes.com/7-of-twitter-users-are-not-human

Taylor, N (2002) 'State surveillance and the right to privacy', *Surveillance & Society*, vol. 1, no. 1, pp.66-85

Tost, LP; Gino, F; Larrick, R (2011) 'Power, competitiveness, and advice taking: why the powerful don't listen', *Organizational Behavior and Human Decision Processes*, vol 117, pp.53-65

Travis, A (2015) 'National Crime Agency must claw back more criminal assets, MPs say', *The Guardian*, www.theguardian.com/uk-news/2015/feb/17/national-crime-agency-criminal-assets-commons-home-affairs-select-committee-nca

Tversky, A and Kahneman, D (1974) 'Judgment under uncertainty: heuristics and biases', *Science*, vol. 185, no. 4157, pp.1124-31

Vessey, W (2010) 'Outstanding leadership', in M. Mumford (ed) *Leadership 101*. Danvers, MA: Springer Publishing

Vinx, L (2007) *Hans Kelsen's Pure Theory of Law, Legality and Legitimacy*. New York, NY: OUP

Waddington, PAJ (2005) 'Slippery slopes and civil libertarian pessimism', *Policing & Society*, vol. 15, no. 3, pp.353-75

Waring, K (2011) 'An examination of the impact of accountability and blame culture on police judgements and decisions in critical incident contexts', Unpublished PhD thesis, University of Liverpool

Ward, P and Horne, A (2015) 'Interception of communications, http://researchbriefings.parliament.uk/ResearchBriefing/Summary/SN06332#fullreport

Westera, N; Kebbell M; Milne, B; Green, T (2014) 'The prospective detective: developing the effective detective of the future', *Policing and Society*, DOI:10.1080/10439463.2014.942845

West Midlands Police Authority (2012) 'Force intelligence update', www.westmidlandspcc.gov.uk/media/203470/10b_pservices_11oct2012_intelligence_update.pdf.

Wheaton, K (2011) 'Who invented the intelligence cycle?', http://sourcesandmethods.blogspot.co.uk/2011/01/rfi-who-invented-intelligence-cycle.html

Williams, D (2015) 'British jihadis in Syria are being recruited for suicide missions to blow up airliners over western cities in "tribute to Osama bin laden"', *Daily Mail*, 10 August, www.dailymail.co.uk/news/article-3192022

Williams, P (1994) *Transnational criminal organisations and international security*. Rand Organisation at https://www.rand.org/content/dam/rand/pubs/monograph_reports/MR880/MR880.ch14.pdf

Williamson, T and Bagshaw, P (2001) 'The ethics of informer handling', in R Billingsley, T Nemitz, and P Bean (eds) *Informers, Policing, Policy, Practice*. Cullompton, Devon: Willan, pp.50-66

Wilson, K and Keelan, J (2013) 'Social media and the empowering of opponents of medical technologies: the case of anti-vaccinationism', *Journal of Medical Internet Research*, vol. 15, no. 5, e103

Winsor, T (2012) *Independent Review of Police Officer and Staff Remuneration and Conditions*. London: HMIC

Zelikow, P (2011) 'Afterword: The twilight war in national commission on terrorist attacks upon the United States', in *The 9/11 Commission Report*. New York, NY: WW Norton and Co, pp.499–548.

Index